Rochester Routes

500. POWERS' BLOCK, ROCHESTER, N. Y.

The Powers Building, c. 1885, photographer unknown

Rochester Routes

Tours of Monroe County's Historic Places

To Ed, Dan and Jay, whose company livens all my journeys.

Patricia Braus

Rochester Routes

Tours of Monroe County's Historic Places

Written by Patricia Braus

Editing and additional research by Ann Parks and Cynthia Howk

Project managed by Flo Paxson

Design, illustration and photography by Frank Petronio

Published by The Landmark Society of Western New York

Support provided by The New York State Council on the Arts and the Gleason Foundation

Rochester Routes: Tours of Monroe County's Historic Places
by Patricia Braus

A publication of the Landmark Society of Western New York
© 2001 by the Landmark Society of Western New York

The information in this book has been carefully
researched and all efforts have been made to ensure
accuracy. The Landmark Society of Western New York
assumes no responsibility for any injuries suffered
or for damages or losses incurred during the use of or
as a direct result of following this information.

If you have any questions or comments concerning
the editorial content of this book, please write to:

The Landmark Society of Western New York
133 South Fitzhugh Street
Rochester, New York 14608

www.landmarksociety.org

Library of Congress Control Number 2001135221
ISBN 0-9641706-7-1

Editing and additional research by Cynthia Howk
and Ann Parks

Flo Paxson, project manager

Lovingly designed, illustrated and produced by
Frank Petronio Design, www.frankpetronio.com

Photography by: Andy Olenick, Hans Padelt,
Frank Petronio, Dawn Tower and several unknown
photographers whose images were found in the
Landmark Society of Western New York archives.

Printed in the U.S.A. on acid-free, recycled paper
using soy-based inks by No Other Impressions
Fine Printing and Finishing, Inc., Rochester
www.nootherimpressions.com

Rochester Routes

Tours of Monroe County's Historic Places

Acknowledgements

This project could not have been completed without the enthusiasm and knowledge of a wonderful collection of individuals who shared their stories with me.

There is Tim O'Connell, who has become the self-taught authority on Frederick Law Olmsted and Rochester's parks. Tim can tell you where Red Creek flowed in Genesee Valley Park 50 years ago and which movie star skated on the Lily Pond in Highland Park (Ingrid Bergman).

There is Anne Bullock, Honeoye Falls historian. "I fell in love with Honeoye Falls the first time I saw it, and I'm still falling in love," she told me at age 88 when we spoke about the village.

And there is Bill Davis, whose passion for the Genesee River led scores of Rochesterians to explore river trails for themselves.

My warm thanks to Landmark Society staffers who labored and drove hundreds of miles on behalf of this project. These include Landmark Society Deputy Executive Director Ann Parks and architectural research coordinator Cynthia Howk, whose professionalism and knowledge were inspiring. I also thank Flo Paxson of the Landmark Society, whose hard work and good sense helped maintain the sanity of everyone involved in this project. Catherine Rourke offered impeccable proofreading skills and solid editorial assistance.

My gratitude also extends to Landmark Society Executive Director Henry McCartney for trusting me with this effort, and Landmark Society trustee Marion A. Simon, who intrigued me with her early description of this project. Trustees Jean Czerkas and Jim Yarrington also were helpful.

I also owe thanks to Vincent Lenti, Kathy Connor, City historian Ruth Rosenberg-Napersteck and Dorothea DeZafra. My thanks also to Bill C.W. Lattin, of the Cobblestone Society; Sister Jean Agnes Michaud and Sister Ann Collins. Also helpful were Jean Geisel, Peter Wisbey, and Shirley DiStefano of the Wheatland Historical Society.

Thanks also to Betty Spencer and Joyce Lobene, who helped identify historic houses in Spencerport, and to Brockport village historian Bill Andrews. I am also grateful to Eunice Chesnut, historian for the Western Monroe Historic Society in Brockport, Ogden historian Shirley Nixon, Brighton historian Mary Jo Lanphear and Pittsford historian Audrey Johnson. My appreciation also to Pat Place of Historic Pittsford, Mendon Town historian Diane Ham and Bob Corby, mayor of Pittsford village and an architect himself.

Special thanks go to Richard Reisem, author of *Erie Canal Legacy* and Karl Kabelac, retired manuscript librarian and archivist at the Rare Books, Special Collections and Preservation Department of the University of Rochester's Rush Rhees Library. They read the book in the intermediate stages and offered good advice and suggestions.

The librarians at the Rundel Library's Local History Division and the staff at the Rochester Historical Society were invaluable.

Many thanks go to my friends Jill Burstein, formerly of Scottsville, Patrice Mitchell, of Rochester, and my son Jay Lopez, who were helpful and entertaining companions on outings during the formation of these routes. My husband Ed Lopez and son, Daniel Lopez, were enthusiastic supporters throughout the project who endured many detours with kindness. Thanks also to my parents Jay and Jane Braus who taught me to take pleasure in good architecture, and to my other supportive family members and friends, who have listened to more than their share of Rochester stories over the past two years.

Finally, I am grateful to the many Rochesterians, past and present, who have committed themselves to maintaining Rochester's architectural heritage, which continues to be threatened in the name of progress. Let this book be a small testimony to the pleasure that can be gained by remembering and preserving the past.

Patricia Braus
October 2001

How Routes Got Started

Rochester Routes: Tours of Monroe County's Historic Places was born more than three years ago. Its genesis was a Landmark Society trustee, Marion Simon who said, "Let's write a book for people like me, who want to learn more about Monroe County's historic places and show them to visitors!" Since people can't walk across the county, we decided to write a driving tour book.

It turned out to be a good idea, but like all spurts of creativity, we still needed to fill in a few thousand details. Our author, Patricia Braus, came on the scene in 1999. By that time, we were pretty sure which routes we wanted the tours to follow, although we changed our minds later. *Rochester Routes* is not comprehensive, and your favorite routes may have been left out. Nevertheless, we hope you will use this book for inspiration, and set out to discover your own *Rochester Routes*.

We are very indebted to the New York State Council on the Arts and the Gleason Foundation, whose support made this book possible.

As Landmark Society staff, we had considerable experience in writing walking tours that cover, with lots of detail, rather small geographic areas. For this book, we had to shift gears, and cover large swaths of geography in an automobile, where conventions like "no left turn" and "one way" mean a lot. We also had to learn to eliminate material, for fear that the book would turn out more like an encyclopedia than a tour guide.

How Rochester Routes is Organized: Chapters, Photos, Maps

Rochester Routes contains five tours, each in its own chapter. Four tours start downtown and proceed to outlying towns and villages, giving a comprehensive look at a portion of Monroe County. The fifth tour starts in Pittsford village and ends in the village of Honeoye Falls. The downtown portion of each tour is an outgrowth of the Landmark Society's earlier publication, *Walking Tours of Downtown Rochester: Images of History.**

At the start of each tour, you'll find mileage information and a list of the places that are open to the public. We have also included a short introduction, so you'll know where you are going to start and finish your tour. Rochester Routes also contains maps to help you follow the tours and point out the properties highlighted in the book.

Because we want you to enjoy reading this book as much as you will enjoy seeing the architecture along the way, we have added a fair amount of historic and anecdotal information; much of it is contained in sidebars so the flow of the tour would not be interrupted. We also have included as many photos as possible so you can easily find the sites described in the text.

Driving Tips

Each tour starts and ends with an area that is ideal for walking. In places like Pittsford village and High Falls in downtown Rochester, the important buildings come up and disappear quickly. You'll enjoy them more if you can slow down. After your walk, you can head for the car.

Because most of each tour will put you behind the wheel, it makes sense to take a navigator with you. As an alternative, we suggest that you read the tour at home before starting out. Although we have chosen sites that are visible from the road, some may go by quickly, so be careful. In some areas, pulling over may not be the best idea, especially during high traffic hours.

Have A Good Time

This book was designed to encourage you to see more, learn more, and appreciate more of Monroe County's architectural heritage. We also hope you will have a good time. Take the pace that suits you best. Drive carefully, look carefully, and take the tours as often as you can to fully enjoy the experience.

Flo Paxson

*You can find these downtown tours from *"Images of History"* on our website. Also on our website is additional information on Monroe County historic and modern places that could not be included in this book. Visit us at *www.landmarksociety.org*

Cultural Rochester
an East Avenue Outing

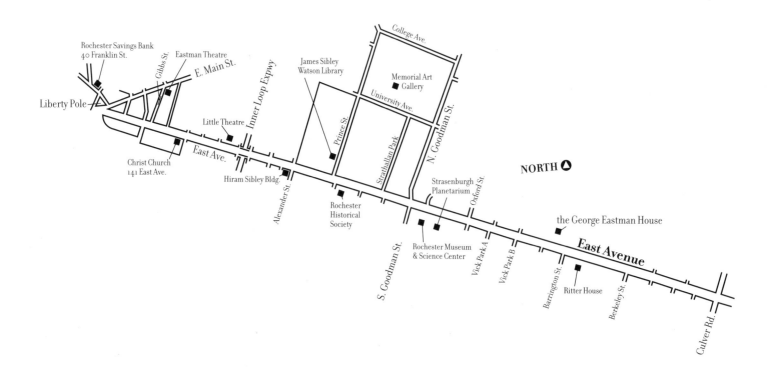

Rochester Savings Bank
40 Franklin St.

Gibbs St.

Eastman Theatre

E. Main St.

Liberty Pole

Inner Loop Expwy

James Sibley
Watson Library

College Ave.

Memorial Art
Gallery

University Ave.

Little Theatre

Prince St.

Strathallan Park

N. Goodman St.

East Ave.

Christ Church
141 East Ave.

Hiram Sibley Bldg.

Alexander St.

Rochester
Historical
Society

NORTH

S. Goodman St.

Strasenburgh
Planetarium

Oxford St.

the George Eastman House

Rochester Museum
& Science Center

Vick Park A

Vick Park B

Barrington St.

Ritter House

Berkeley St.

East Avenue

Culver Rd.

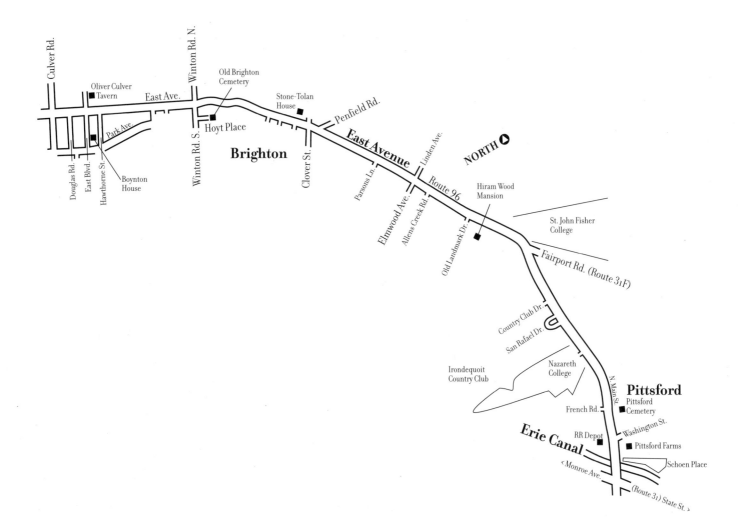

Culver Rd.

Oliver Culver
Tavern

East Ave.

Winton Rd. N.

Old Brighton
Cemetery

Stone-Tolan
House

Park Ave.

Winton Rd. S.

Hoyt Place

Penfield Rd.

East Avenue

Douglas Rd.

East Blvd.

Hawthorne St.

Boynton
House

Brighton

Clover St.

NORTH

Parsons Ln.

Elmwood Ave.

Allens Creek Rd.

Route 96

Linden Ave.

Hiram Wood
Mansion

Old Landmark Dr.

St. John Fisher
College

Fairport Rd. (Route 31F)

Country Club Dr.

San Rafael Dr.

Irondequoit
Country Club

Nazareth
College

N. Main St.

Pittsford

Pittsford
Cemetery

French Rd.

Washington St.

Erie Canal

RR Depot

Pittsford Farms

Schoen Place

< Monroe Ave.

(Route 31) State St. >

This tour begins at the Liberty Pole in downtown Rochester and proceeds along East Avenue to Pittsford, ending at Schoen Place.

Mileage: Approximately 11 miles

Time: Approximately 1½ hours

~ Open to the Public ~

Rochester Historical Society
485 East Avenue, phone 271-2705

Memorial Art Gallery
500 University Avenue, phone 473-7720

George Eastman House,
900 East Avenue, phone 271-3361

Rochester Museum & Science Center
657 East Avenue, phone 271-4320

Stone-Tolan House Museum
2370 East Avenue, phone 442-4606

It is an early spring morning in 1908, and George Eastman, founder of Eastman Kodak Company, rises on the second floor of his East Avenue mansion to dress for breakfast. Downstairs, an organist slips quietly into Eastman's three-year-old Georgian home. He strides past the just budding elm trees shipped here full-grown by Erie Canal barge. At precisely 7:30 a.m., the musician settles at the massive Aeolian organ in the conservatory. The sound vibrating through the thousand-pipe organ begins on schedule, just as Eastman is walking downstairs for breakfast in the conservatory.

It is unlikely that any of the current residents of East Avenue use an organist playing a made-to-order, $30,000 pipe organ for breakfast accompaniment. Yet such grand gestures have long had a home on East Avenue.

For decades, East Avenue has served as Rochester's finest boulevard, a place of elegance and style. From behind facades of limestone, stucco and brick, the city's elite have forged lives and helped mold the community. Though some historic buildings have been lost, the avenue has retained most of its landmarks, and remains an architectural showplace.

The story of East Avenue's development is the story of the men and women who built Rochester, including such luminaries as Eastman and Western Union founder Hiram Sibley. Yet it also is the story of the follies and dreams of these same leaders and others, men and women who built everything from a horse race track to an astronomical observatory along the avenue.

East Avenue started as an Indian trail, and was widened to become a road in 1805-1806 by early settlers Oliver Culver (the first superintendent of Brighton), Orringh Stone, and three other men. The men cut the road four miles, from Stone's tavern (now the Stone-Tolan House Museum in Brighton, owned by the Landmark Society of Western New York) west to the Genesee River. They received a total of $50 for the job from the early town of Northfield. Rochester was settled after Pittsford and Brighton, making today's trip from Rochester to Pittsford an eleven-mile route back in time.

This route leads from the Liberty Pole Triangle downtown east on East Avenue to Pittsford, with a small detour through Rochester's "Neighborhood of the Arts," that includes the original University of Rochester campus.

The brief downtown section of this tour is possible by car, but would be best done by foot, starting at Franklin Street, just north of the intersection of East Main and Franklin streets. Rochester's first business area was at the west end of downtown, at what today is called the Four Corners. But the downtown area near the Liberty Triangle quickly became a vital part of the community as Rochester grew in the middle 1800s.

The original Liberty Pole, built in 1846 as a monument to a young community's patriotism, was constructed of wood only 35 years after Colonel Nathaniel Rochester began selling property in what would become Rochester. On the other hand, the current **Liberty Pole**, built in 1965, is a steel monument to Rochester's resilience. This pole is the latest of three Liberty

Poles to grace this downtown location. The first two fell down, with the second toppling in a windstorm the day after Christmas in 1889. Seventy years later, the present Liberty Pole, designed by Rochester architect James H. Johnson, was constructed.

The Liberty Pole Triangle area is marked by many distinguished buildings, most built in the late 19th and early 20th centuries. Just north of the Liberty Pole is the former Rochester Savings Bank building at **40 Franklin Street**, now Charter One Bank. Designed by McKim, Mead and White (see sidebar, this chapter), the pre-eminent New York firm of the time, with Rochester's J. Foster Warner (see sidebar, Chapter 2), the 1929 building is an example of 20th-century Byzantine style. The outside is handsome, featuring majestic arched windows and elegant columns, but the understated exterior masks the lush beauty of the interior. Rouge antique marble columns and a painted ceiling by American muralist Ezra Winter are among the treasures inside. The majestic wall mosaic was produced at the Ravenna Studios in Berlin from Winter's designs, complete with the bank's motto at the time: "Industry and Thrift are the Foundations of Prosperity."

From Franklin Street, cross over Main Street onto East Avenue. Immediately on the left, the Sibley Triangle Building, at **20-26 East Avenue**, was designed by J. Foster Warner more than three decades earlier. Constructed in 1897, the triangle-shaped building contains Neoclassical and Romanesque design features such as large brick arches and Roman-arched windows on the 5th floor. The building was constructed for Hiram W. Sibley, a philanthropist, banker, real estate agent, and heir to the fortune amassed by his father, Hiram Sibley, founder of Western Union Telegraph Company.

The next building on the left, the Cutler Building, at **42 East Avenue**, also was built in 1897. This Italianate-style building with a copper-covered tower was designed and owned by James G. Cutler, one of Rochester's Renaissance men, the architect, inventor and later mayor of Rochester. As inventor and manufacturer of the mail chute, Cutler had traveled the world prior to his election as mayor in the early 1900s. One of his many accomplishments as mayor was construction of the first public playground at Brown's Square.

To view the **Eastman Theatre** at **435 East Main Street**, take a left on Gibbs Street. The theater, which opened in 1922, is on your right.

Perhaps the best-known monument to Rochester culture, the theater is East Avenue's downtown cultural anchor, a testimony to George Eastman's massive influence on Rochester life. A passionate music lover, Eastman donated the theater to the University of Rochester and personally supervised its construction. The building, which ultimately cost Eastman over $3 million, is a Neoclassical design. Sumptuous outside, it features a curved facade with recessed Ionic columns and a canopy stretching the length of the building. Inside, the theater is also richly decorated with murals by Barry Faulkner and Ezra Winter. A reproduction of the much-loved Maxfield Parrish painting, Interlude, has replaced the original (now at the Memorial Art Gallery) in the theater.

The unorthodox layout of the Eastman Theatre stems from George Eastman's hard-nosed pragmatism. While most theater lobbies are rectangular and lead directly back to the theater itself, the Eastman is more L-shaped than symmetrical. Entry to the theater is skewed to

Eastman Theatre, 435 East Main Street   *Olenick*

one side of the lobby. The layout was dictated by the site, which in turn was dictated by a stubborn neighbor. Originally, Eastman wanted to acquire more property for the new theater. But the owner of a building on the corner of Main and Swan (now demolished) asked too high a price, and Eastman refused to pay, choosing instead to change the plans. This situation infuriated the famous primary architects McKim, Mead and White, the firm that collaborated on the project with local architectural firm Gordon and Kaelber. When McKim, Mead and White heard about the adjustment of the plan to fit the new space, it pulled out of the project for a time. The firm agreed to continue – as long as it was made clear in publicity accounts that McKim, Mead and White was not credited with the floor plans.

After viewing the theater, take a right on Main Street, then an immediate right on Swan Street, and a left onto East Avenue. Immediately on your right is one of the earliest churches in Rochester, **Christ Church**, at **141 East Avenue**. Designed by British architect Robert Gibson, this 1892 Gothic Revival building replaced an earlier, smaller Episcopal church erected on this site in 1855. The present structure retains the sanctuary and a portion of the nave from the original church. In 1902, the bell tower was added. The 1892 sanctuary was designed by Tiffany Studios artist Frederick Wilson and features two opalescent glass windows. Wilson also designed the mosaic wall behind the altar of white Italian marble.

Continuing along East Avenue, one encounters on the left two of the best examples of Art Deco architecture in Rochester: the former Hallman's Chevrolet Building at **200 East Avenue**, and **the Little Theatre** at **240 East Avenue**. Hallman's was built in the early part of the 20th century as an auto dealership and showroom, and completely remodeled in the 1930s with Art Deco features such as gleaming black structural glass, a large arched window, stainless steel, and neon signs and clock. This city-designated landmark has been revitalized with a new commercial tenant in the former auto showroom and the construction of contemporary townhouses to the rear of the building. Since opening in 1929, the Little Theatre has graced East Avenue with its black glazed exterior, Art Deco marquee, and frieze of silver baked on terra cotta. Designed by Rochester architect Edgar Phillips, the theater has remained in continuous use as a venue for art films.

Proceed east to the corner of Alexander Street. Here, the Hiram Sibley Building at **311 Alexander Street** on the right, and its companion across the street, the Fitch Building, **315 Alexander Street**, serve as a traditional gateway between the business and residential areas of East Avenue. Built a mere four years before the Little Theatre, the Hiram Sibley Building's Neoclassical and Italian Renaissance style is a world apart.

Designed to resemble a wing of Hampden Court Palace outside of London, the brick-with-limestone trimmed building is the work of the noted Boston firm of Shepley, Bulfinch and Abbot. It features numerous sculptural enhancements and a richly detailed pediment above second- and third-story Corinthian columns. The pediment and other details can best be seen by parking on the other side of Alexander Street or a short distance up East Avenue.

Also visible from the corner of East Avenue and Alexander Street is the distinctive Alexandrian Apartment building to the right at **300 Alexander Street**. Directly across the street from the Hiram Sibley Building, this handsome brick edifice was designed in 1906 by architect J. Foster Warner, and originally served as a dormitory for the

Hiram Sibley Building, 311 Alexander Street   *Olenick*

Rochester Theological Seminary, located on this site until 1928. After the seminary closed, the chapel and classroom buildings to the north were demolished and the surviving dormitory converted into apartments.

At Home on East Avenue

After leaving the East Avenue of commerce, the East Avenue of gracious living emerges. Here, along a mile-and-a-half-long corridor, is one of the most important collections of 19th- and early-20th-century urban residential architecture in New York state. Immediately on the left is the Hiram Sibley House at **400 East Avenue**. Built in 1868 by Hiram Sibley, president of Western Union and then the wealthiest man in Rochester, the house was originally Italianate in style, with a cupola and bracketed details, and sat on a spacious, multi-acre lot. In the early 20th century, however, Sibley's grandson remodeled the house in the Georgian Revival style. A Sibley family residence until 1975, it was subsequently adapted for commercial use.

Woodside, 485 East Avenue   *Lodder*

When the first mansions were constructed on East Avenue in the late 1830s and early 1840s, Rochester was a newly settled community, basking in the success of the Erie Canal, which had opened to Rochester in 1823.

Nathaniel Hawthorne wrote about the influx of travelers to the area in an account first published in 1835: "The porters were lumbering up the steps with baggage from the packet boats, while waiters plied the brush on dusty travelers who, meanwhile, glanced over the innumerable advertisements in the daily papers."

But there also were frightening challenges in building a new settlement. A deadly cholera epidemic killed 400 to 500 people in the summer of 1832. Eager to establish their families at this exciting and sometimes threatening time, a trio of early businessmen constructed the first mansions on East Avenue around 1840. These elegant houses, at **Nos. 421, 474** and **485 East Avenue**, summoned up the solidity and permanence of ancient culture, using the popular Greek Revival style. At the time, East Avenue was at the edge of the developing city. Mansions already crowded the Third Ward, now known as Corn Hill, and families who wanted space and land moved to East Avenue.

On the right, across the street from the Hiram Sibley House, is the Aaron Erickson House at **421 East Avenue**. Completed in 1842, this early Greek Revival residence was later known as the Perkins House. It has been the home of the Genesee Valley Club since the early 20th century.

Just past No. 421, on the right, is Woodside at **485 East Avenue**. Located on the corner of Sibley Place, it is the most prominent of the trio of neighboring Greek Revival mansions. Built from 1838-1841 by architect-builder Alfred M. Badger, the house features a striking round turret on top of a square cupola, and has a massive entrance porch graced by Doric columns. A series of decorative wrought iron grilles stretch across the frieze band. Built for storekeeper Silas O. Smith, his wife Seba Hand Ward Smith and their six children, Woodside retains much of its elegant 19th-century interior detail. The headquarters and museum of the **Rochester Historical Society** since 1941, the mansion is open to the public.

Though East Avenue today is highly developed, its isolation in the late 1840s drove the early owners of the Pitkin House, at **474 East Avenue**, directly across the street from Woodside, to move back to the more populous Third Ward. Even by the late 1880s, the area had enough space to allow the Hiram Sibley estate at 400 East Avenue to house goats and a cart in the park-like back yard as a way to entertain children.

Turn left on Strathallan Park, a street of elegant late-19th- and early-20th-century houses. Turn left again on University Avenue for a small detour through Rochester's "Neighborhood of the Arts." This is a tour through one of the city's most distinctive neighborhoods, which includes the original campus of the University of Rochester, on the north side of University Avenue, between North Goodman and Prince streets. The university was founded as a men's college in 1850 in the old United States Hotel on Buffalo Street, now West Main Street (see Chapter 4). Beginning in 1861, the school constructed its first academic building on a large parcel between Prince and Goodman streets, framed by College and University avenues. At this location, the university was in the heart of a growing metropolis.

In 1930, the College for Men of the University of Rochester moved to its current location south of downtown on the Genesee River (see Chapter 3), though the College for Women remained at Prince Street until 1955.

To see the University of Rochester's original building on this campus, take a right on Prince Street and another right on College Avenue. On the right stands Anderson Hall, completed in 1861, at **75 College Avenue**. Designed by Boston architect Alexander R. Esty, it housed the offices and classrooms of the University of Rochester during the 1860s. Constructed of Medina sandstone, the building features a polychrome, slate mansard roof and tall, arched windows.

To return to the tour, turn right on North Goodman Street and right on University Avenue. On the right are two of the more prominent university buildings: **the Memorial Art Gallery, 500 University Avenue**, a Neoclassical edifice constructed in 1913 with additions in 1926, 1968 and 1987, and the attached **Cutler Union**, built in 1932-33, and named in honor of former mayor, architect and inventor, James G. Cutler. The shot sawn limestone Cutler Union, with its 135-foot Gothic tower and stained glass Gothic windows, was designed by the Rochester architectural firm of Gordon and Kaelber. Other former university buildings here include the former Munro Hall, which now is part of the City School District's **School of the Arts** at **45 Prince Street**.

Turning left on Prince Street, one sees on the left **8-10 Prince Street**, the monumental building and campus that is the former Sacred Heart Academy. Established in 1845, it includes several additions constructed in the late-19th- and early-20th-centuries. Finely detailed with red brick and stained glass windows, the complex includes several architectural styles. The square, brick Italianate style building (1845) on the far right is joined by a Second Empire-style main building (1874) with mansard roof, and a distinctive stone Gothic chapel (1890), the design of Chicago architect, Adolphus Druiding.

Across the street from the former Academy are two remarkable residential buildings. The James Sibley Watson Library at **9 Prince Street**, set back from the road, is one of the region's more idio-syncratic buildings. Built in 1903 and designed by New York architect John du Fais, it is modeled after the Petit Trianon Palace at Versailles. This private residence features delicate and finely detailed brick, terra cotta, cut stone, and a glass-enclosed conservatory. The elegant structure is the surviving wing of an 1878 house. Built by Hiram Sibley for his daughter Emily, the original house was demolished in the 1950s. The library

James Sibley Watson Library, 9 Prince Street   *Padelt*

Strasenburgh Planetarium, 663 East Avenue   *Padelt*

wing interior features elaborate woodwork and a painted ceiling created by artist and architectural designer Harvey Ellis. Ellis is best known for his American Arts and Crafts-style furnishings, but he also designed the Lamberton House, 737 East Avenue, and Grace Episcopal Church in Scottsville. (For more on Harvey Ellis, see Chapter 3.)

Next door to the Watson Library is a picturesque house at **7 Prince Street**, designed by Rochester architect, John R. Thomas, and built in 1878 on the property of attorney William Cogswell, who erected this house as a wedding present for his daughter. Remotely derived from the Gothic Revival, but with something of the character of Eastlake, it is an imaginative work well representing the 1870s.

Also on the right, set at the corner of East Avenue, is the **First Church of Christ Scientist, 440 East Avenue**. Built on the former site of the Cogswell family's 1850s home, this Beaux Arts-style structure exhibits a strong Italian Renaissance influence. Designed by Rochester architects Gordon and Kaelber, the church was begun in the fall of 1914 and completed in 1916 at a cost of approximately $250,000.

To continue the tour, take a left turn onto East Avenue. On your right, at the **corner of East Avenue and Meigs Street**, is the imposing campus of **Third Presbyterian Church**, built in 1893 from designs by Orlando K. Foote in the Neo-Romanesque style associated with the previous decade. Immediately east of the church is **Arnold Park**. Laid out in the 1850s as a private street, Arnold Park is an early urban counterpart to today's "gated" communities. Note the formal entryway to the street, with masonry, gate posts and balustrade, now designated city landmarks.

On the southwest corner of East Avenue and Arnold Park (present site of the Third Presbyterian Chapel, built in the 1950s), a world-renowned observatory was erected in 1879 by H. H. Warner, who earned a fortune selling patent medicine.

At the corner of East Avenue and Goodman Street, you will see on your right the large campus of the **Rochester Museum and Science Center, 657-663 East Avenue**. Originally located on the west side of the city in Edgerton Park (see Chapter 2), the museum moved to this site in the 1940s, when the Bausch family donated their property to the growing institution. In 1968, the **Strasenburgh Planetarium**, one of the modern landmarks of

Monroe County, was built on the campus from a design executed by Rochester architects, Waasdorp, Northrup and Kaelber.

Across the street from the museum campus at **666 East Avenue** is one of the few Gothic Revival works in the neighborhood. Built about 1852-54 of Medina sandstone, salvaged from the original canal aqueduct across the Genesee River, the house was erected by Charles F. Bissell, who constructed the second Erie Canal aqueduct (now the Broad Street Bridge).

Next door to the planetarium, on the right, is the Strong-Todd House, **693 East Avenue**, built in 1901 for Colonel Henry A. Strong, president of Eastman Kodak Company. Designed by Rochester architect J. Foster Warner, this large brick and stone residence illustrates the taste of the decade following the Chicago World's Fair.

Also on your right, at the corner of East Avenue and Oxford Street, is **No. 737**, one of the many outstanding and unusual residences along the avenue. Built in 1883 and designed by Harvey Ellis, it was originally the home of Alexander Lamberton, the first head of the Rochester Park System. Its pleasing composition reflects the designs of English architect Richard Norman Shaw, and includes a trio of two-story bay windows and striking small-paned windows lighting the interior, three-story stairwell.

By the late 1880s and early 1900s, affluence ruled the day on East Avenue. One woman, for example, reported that as a child, her household employed three butlers, three gardeners, two chauffeurs, one cook, one laundress, two upstairs maids, and a personal maid for her mother. Such stories help explain the large scale of many of East Avenue's houses.

On the right, **Vick Park A** and **Vick Park B** recall the horticultural heritage of the city and this neighborhood, in particular, when James Vick developed his nursery business here in the mid-19th century. In 1855, a horse race course was built at the south end of the present streets (today, the curved section of Park Avenue). By the 1870s, Vick Parks A and B were laid out and houses developed on the former Vick nursery grounds.

With its imposing tower, **St. Paul's Episcopal Church**, on the right, continues the tradition of the Gothic style for houses of worship. Located opposite the Eastman House at **41 Westminster Road**, this stately church was built in 1897 from the design of Heins and LaFarge of New York.

On the left, just past Portsmouth Terrace, is the palatial mansion of George Eastman, completed in 1905 at **900 East Avenue**. Open to the public, the house is part of an enlarged museum, the **George Eastman House**, which includes the restored mansion and the International Museum of Photography and Film. Designed by McKim, Mead and White in collaboration with local architect J. Foster Warner, the Georgian Revival building has four free-standing Corinthian columns at the front doorway, six chimneys and an elaborate pediment above the entryway.

Construction was supervised almost daily by George Eastman, who had theories about every aspect of building a house. For example, he believed that porte cocheres, covered entryways, are "ugly at best," and beamed ceilings are unnecessary. In his own home, he stopped workmen using a mechanical sander on the floors because he was not satisfied with the results. Instead, they sanded the floors on all fours to accent the grain of the butterfly-joined teak and parqueted oak. In 1919, the rear portion of the

McKim, Mead and White

The New York City architectural firm of McKim, Mead and White is a major figure on this tour of East Ave. With the help of local architects, the firm designed the George Eastman House in 1905, the Eastman Theatre in 1922 and the Rochester Savings Bank in 1929.

Throughout the late 1800s and early 1900s, McKim, Mead and White transformed American architecture, specializing in monumental public buildings. The firm's buildings featured Greek, Roman and Renaissance detail. Famous buildings designed by the firm include the Morgan Library, Low Memorial Library at Columbia University and the Boston Public Library.

The well-known partners in the firm included the colorful Stanford White (1853-1906). He was murdered by millionaire Harry Kendall Thaw, the husband of actress Evelyn Nesbit, with whom White had had an affair. White was shot on the roof garden of the first Madison Square Garden, a building he designed. Other partners in the firm included Charles Follen McKim (1847-1909) and William Rutherford Mead (1846-1928). By 1900, there were over 100 architects in the firm.

George Eastman House, 1972   *Padelt*

house was moved back in order to enlarge the music room, which contains an organ, an instrument of which Eastman was especially fond. The George Eastman House opened as a museum in 1949. A grand staircase marks the interior, which has been restored to reflect Eastman's graciously opulent lifestyle.

Just past Barrington Street on the right, the Ritter House at **947 East Avenue** is visible with its monumental round tower and tile roof. Built in 1907 for industrialist Frank Ritter, the house was designed by architect Leon Stern to resemble castles in Ritter's native Bavaria. Also on the right, the picturesque and eclectic Alexander Lindsay House, constructed in 1878, is located at **973 East Avenue**. One of the oldest mansions standing east of Goodman Street, this brick residence was built by a founder of the Sibley, Lindsay and Curr Company Department store for his family, who remained here until the 1920s.

As you approach Berkeley Street, on the right, a large copper beech tree planted in 1870 marks the Italianate-style Spencer House at **1005 East Avenue**, which was built in 1865 and remodeled by J. Foster Warner in the early 1900s. The exten-

Ritter House, 947 East Avenue   *Tower*

sive grounds also feature notable landscaping and gardens developed during the mid-20th century by former owners, Harriet and Thomas Spencer.

Another important house on East Avenue is the mansion at **No. 1050**, the former Soule House, on the left, near the corner of Granger Place. Now owned by **Asbury First United Methodist Church**, it once was slated for demolition. Designed by J. Foster Warner and built of textured buff Indiana limestone in 1892, the Richardson Romanesque house has a sculptural richness seen most notably in the study, which features a profusion of delicately hand-carved teak with a gold filigree ceiling. Though the house was built for Wilson Soule, the son of the founder of the Hop Bitters Patent Medicine Company, Soule and his family lived there only two years. The house was purchased by George Eastman, who lived there until his mansion was completed in 1905, adding such improvements as an indoor shooting gallery and a photography laboratory in the basement.

Continue east to the intersection of East Avenue and Culver Road, named for pioneer settler Oliver Culver, who built his house and tavern here in 1816.

On the immediate right at **1209 East Avenue** is the imposing Colonial Revival-style residence constructed in 1903 for Kodak executive, Walter S. Hubbell, and designed by architect J. Foster Warner. Diagonally across the street, on the left, the large brick house with extensive lawns at **1250 East Avenue** was designed for plumbing supply executive, William E. Sloan, whose family continued to live here for seven decades. Designed by architect Claude Bragdon in 1906, the house is an example of Colonial Revival architecture and features a distinctive bowfront facade. (For more on Bragdon, see Chapter 3)

Just past Culver Road, turn right on **Douglas Road**. Developed in the 1920s and '30s, this street of fine Colonial Revival- and Tudor-style houses still conveys a sense of early 20th-century residential design. At the end of Douglas Road, turn left on Park Avenue, then immediately left on East Boulevard.

Two of the most significant residences in the area are located here on East Boulevard, a small street that intersects with East Avenue just east of Culver Road. The third house on the right is the Boynton House, at **16 East Boulevard**. Built in 1907-08, this early Prairie-style residence is Rochester's only Frank Lloyd Wright-designed house.

Frank Lloyd Wright House — 16 East Boulevard

The Frank Lloyd Wright house at 16 East Boulevard should be immediately recognizable to admirers of the man who is perhaps the best known 20th-century architect. The Prairie-style house, with its characteristic separated planes and broad horizontal lines, was built in 1907-1908, when Wright was a young man in his 30s.

The house, praised by architectural historian Paul Malo for its "floating quality," features broad overhanging eaves and richly detailed leaded glass.

An account by George T. Swan, whose father was contractor for the building, described Wright's eccentric behavior. Even when there was no roof on the house, Swan reported, Wright slept during a rainy spell under a makeshift lean-to, eating cold carrots and turning down offers of hot meals and companionship.

Edward Boynton, who commissioned the house, was a lantern manufacturer. "People thought it was revolutionary, and the most frequent comment I heard was that it was a style of architecture that wouldn't last," reported Edward's daughter, Beulah Boynton, in a 1959 newspaper article.

Boynton House, 16 East Boulevard　　　　　*Padelt*

Continue north on East Boulevard, cross East Avenue, and look to the right, just beyond the first house, where you will see the Oliver Culver Tavern at **No. 70**. One of the most notable Federal-style residences in western New York, this frame, clapboard building was constructed in 1816 as a combination inn and private house. Festivities at the inn were celebrated in the second floor ballroom, which was built with a special spring floor that stretched across the full width of the house. Originally located at the corner of East Avenue and Culver Road, this landmark was moved to East Boulevard in 1906.

Return to East Avenue and turn left. Look for another distinguished house on the right, **1399 East Avenue**, on the corner of Hawthorne Street. Originally built in 1856 as part of a suburban estate, the Bates-Ryder House resembles an Italian villa. With its square tower and low-pitched roofs, the residence still includes four acres of grounds and gardens. One of the largest houses on East Avenue, it has been divided into condominiums.

Next door, on the right, the Academy of Medicine has been located in the Lyon family's mansion at **1441 East Avenue** since 1938. The

1545 East Avenue between 1886 and 1915

home of one of Rochester's most prominent families, the original house on this site, built in 1860, was greatly enlarged to its present 33-room size in 1910. Its design reflects English Tudor and Jacobean style architecture.

Also on the right, the house at **1545 East Avenue** is the Chateauesque-style residence built in 1879 for the family of W. W. Chapin. Original landscape features of this picturesque site include a winding stream and stone bridge.

Early Brighton

The commercial neighborhood where East Avenue intersects Winton Road offers few clues to the historical riches of the location. While the East Avenue-Winton Road intersection is now located within the city, from 1818 to 1905 it was part of the independent village of Brighton. During that period, Brighton was not the developed suburban town it is today. With the Erie Canal extending along what is now Interstate 490, the village of Brighton was a drinking mecca, and included a number of taverns patronized by canal workers. In the middle 1840s, taverns occupied three of the four corners at the Winton Road and East Avenue intersection. The so-called "canawlers" stopped for drinks as their boats were laboriously lifted or lowered through the three locks of the canal. Tavern owner William Bloss is best remembered for his dramatic tossing of all the liquor in his bar into the canal when he had the revelation that alcohol was evil. Determined to improve the world, Bloss organized Monroe County's first anti-slavery convention in 1834.

On your right, before the intersection with Winton Road, is the stone-built **Brighton Presbyterian Church** at **1783 East Avenue**, one of the few remaining historic buildings near the intersection of East Avenue and Winton Road. Since 1872, this church has been an oasis of greenery in this commercial district. Founded as the Brighton Congregational Church in 1817, the church held its first service at Orringh Stone's tavern, now the front room of the Landmark Society's Stone-Tolan House Museum at 2370 East Avenue, located a mile east of the church.

Take a short detour to see the old **Brighton Cemetery**, which overlooks the expressway. To view the cemetery, take a right at Winton Road, drive over Interstate 490, immediately turn left onto **Hoyt Place**, a short, dead-end street. At the end of Hoyt Place are two remarkable, early-19th-century properties, which originally overlooked the Erie Canal (now the Route 490 Expressway). With its two acres of landscaped grounds, the imposing brick house on the right at **45 Hoyt Place** dates from the early 19th century and includes both Greek Revival- and Federal-style details. Next door, the cemetery, with its picturesque entryway, is the resting place of many of Brighton's earliest settlers, including Orringh Stone and William Bloss. For much of the 19th century, the original Brighton Presbyterian Church was also located here on Hoyt Place, next to the cemetery. After a disastrous fire, it relocated to its present site on East Avenue in the 1870s.

To return to the tour, take a right onto Winton Road, then a right on East Avenue and resume the drive to Brighton and Pittsford. To the left beyond the Route 490 overpass, at **Nos. 2280, 2290 and 2300**, are three early-20th-century, Colonial Revival houses, now commercial office buildings. They are the remnants of early-20th-century suburban development, much of which was demolished in the 1960s for the construction of the Route 490 Expressway.

On the left, the white fence marks the four-acre property that includes the **Stone-Tolan House Museum** at **2370 East Avenue**. Owned and operated by the Landmark Society of Western New York as a house museum, it is believed to be the oldest building still standing in Monroe County. The home, also used as a tavern, was built close to the Council Rock, a prominent Seneca Indian landmark at the intersection of two trails. Later, the Council Rock was moved to the Stone-Tolan property and is now located on East Avenue, opposite Council Rock Avenue.

The Stone-Tolan House, built in 1792 by Orringh and Elizabeth Stone, served as an anchor for a young community. In 1814, for instance, the tavern hosted the town of Brighton's first meeting. Famous guests who stayed there included Aaron Burr, the former United States vice president who killed Alexander Hamilton in a duel in 1804. The house, now open to the public, is surrounded by orchards and gardens, and boasts an authentically preserved interior that includes a large cooking fireplace, wide plank floors and period furniture. The exterior features delicate moldings and wood corner quoins.

Stone-Tolan House, 2370 East Avenue   *Petronio*

Though the area around the house is now fully developed, this was not the case in the 19th and early 20th centuries. The late Ellen A. Tolan, who grew up in the house, was interviewed for a mid-1950s newspaper story. "It's more pleasant now than it was then," she said. "It used to be all woods and dark and kind of lonesome."

Just past the Stone-Tolan House, a cluster of apartment buildings along East Avenue marks the beginning of suburban Brighton. Though the Brighton area was settled early, most of its residential neighborhoods were developed in the early 20th century, when the area grew dramatically, following the first appearance, around 1900, of automobiles and an interurban trolley line. This section of the route, from Penfield Road to the village of Pittsford, is generously landscaped and features many large houses with majestic grounds. A low stone wall on the right, a rare 19th-century roadside remnant, leads to the Parsons-Kingston House at **2855 East Avenue**, located on the corner of Parsons Lane. This is the oldest surviving building on the stretch of East Avenue between Penfield Road and Elmwood Avenue. Constructed between 1872-1873, the residence was built by the Parsons family, who were prominent, early-19th-century settlers involved in agriculture and milling along Allen's Creek. The family's large farm encompassed extensive acreage, including land that is now Corbett's Glen and the Country Club of Rochester. The clapboard residence reflects 19th-century vernacular design, a mode of building based on regional forms and materials. Note the Gothic Revival windows with pointed arches on top.

Continue east on East Avenue. At the intersection of Allens Creek Road, you will cross a stone bridge over Allens Creek. For much of the 19th-century, the creek was a major industrial site with grist, saw, and gun powder mills along its banks. The last surviving mill in the neighborhood, the Parsons-Barnes Mill on the north side of Linden Avenue, was demolished in the 1960s during the construction of the Route 490 Expressway.

Just past Old Landmark Drive on your right and set back from the road, is a substantial Georgian Revival house at **3497 East Avenue**. Built in 1907 and now owned by the Basilian Fathers, a Catholic order of priests, this mansion, with its extensive grounds, was first owned by lawyer Hiram R. Wood. A well known politician and auto aficionado,

Wood owned one of the earliest electric cars in the area. Wood's foray into national politics was disastrous, as he died in New York City in 1920 while campaigning for a seat in the United States Congress.

Bear to the right at the fork in the road, as East Avenue continues towards Pittsford. The campus of **St. John Fisher College**, **3690 East Avenue**, founded in 1951, is on the left.

Turn right on Country Club Drive and stop to view two neighboring houses designed by Claude Bragdon. On the right, at the corner of East Avenue and Country Club Drive, is a Colonial Revival house at **3901 East Avenue**. Originally built as a farmhouse in 1830, it included property that now encompasses land owned by Oak Hill Country Club and Irondequoit Country Club. In 1910, the house was remodeled and expanded by Claude Bragdon. Today, this sprawling and finely detailed residence features a curved, free-standing interior staircase and an Adirondack-style gazebo on the grounds.

Across the street to your left, on the opposite corner at **3939 East Avenue**, is another Claude Bragdon-designed residence. This 1909 Classical

Revival house features two massive columns on the facade and a central entrance with a balcony above the front door.

Turn around and return to East Avenue. Turn right on East Avenue, then take the next right on San Rafael Drive, an attractive side street that will loop back onto East Avenue. One of the first suburban residential streets in the neighborhood, San Rafael Drive features a number of distinctive, early-20th-century houses. One of the most notable examples of Mediterranean Revival residential design in the area is the house on the left at **15 San Rafael Drive**. Built in the mid-1930s, this picturesque residence features a tile roof, arched loggia and courtyard. The original owner, head of the physics depart at Kodak's research laboratory, viewed this style of architecture on a European trip and decided to build his Rochester home to resemble an Italian villa.

The work of innovative Syracuse architect Ward Wellington Ward is evident in the mid-1920s houses he designed at **Nos. 12, 20, and 22 San Rafael Drive**, visible on your right. Here, the characteristics of the Arts and Crafts style are shown with the use of stucco, stone, leaded glass and Moravian tiles.

Return to East Avenue and turn right. The campus of **Nazareth College** at **4141 East Avenue** opened in 1942, replacing the college's Augustine Street campus on the west side of Rochester. Originally a women's college, Nazareth was founded in 1924 by the Sisters of Saint Joseph. The campus includes a number of distinguished buildings, including Smyth Hall, the main administration building erected in 1942 with its tall, Gothic Revival tower. On the hilltop to the right, just past the entrance to the College Arts Center, is the 1925 stone and wood French House, "La Maison Francaise," located at **4247 East Avenue**. This Colonial Revival residence, once used as a hunter's retreat and fox barn, is distinguished by its slate roof and richly detailed stone and wood trim.

Just past the college campus, on the right, two fine Craftsman-type Bungalows with sloping roofs can be found on the right at **Nos. 4383 and 4401**. The 1920 house at No. 4383 features stucco with wood trim, Japanese-inspired wood porch columns on stucco piers, and a tile roof. The 1910 house at No. 4401 includes brick, stucco and wood cladding, with a flared roof supported by large stucco columns. In the early 1900s, houses like these were promoted as easily affordable, and could be built for around $1,000.

Just south of French Road, as you enter the historic village of Pittsford, East Avenue becomes North Main Street. At the entrance to the village, on the left, is the **Pittsford Cemetery**. Established in the 1840s, the cemetery's hilly terrain, varied funerary architecture and sugar maple-lined roadways reflect the Rural Cemetery Movement of the mid-19th century.

After you drive under the railroad overpass, on your left at **44 North Main Street** you will see a large Italianate house set on a knoll behind a cast-iron fence. Known as Pittsford Farms, the house is part of a mid-19th-century farm estate retaining cast-iron statuary, park-like grounds, an extensive collection of outbuildings, and agricultural lands. During the 19th century, the farm was the home of several of Pittsford's most prominent citizens and gained national acclaim for its prize-winning herds of Shetland ponies and Jersey cattle. Today, Pittsford Farms is listed in the National Register of Historic Places. The property remains an active family-owned

business, including a produce farming operation and a dairy, which still sells milk in returnable glass bottles. This farm is one of eight farms in the community preserved for the enjoyment of future generations by the Town of Pittsford's purchase of development rights.

Across the street, to the right, at **41 North Main Street**, the former Auburn line of the New York Central Railroad passenger and freight depots, constructed in the late 19th century, now form part of a modern hotel complex.

One of the village of Pittsford's most popular places to visit is the scenic Erie Canal waterfront along **Schoen Place** (pronounced "shane"), located on the left, just past Pittsford Farms. Turn here to end this driving tour and to enjoy the ambience of this quaint and historic, canal-side shopping area. From the time the canal opened in 1824 until well into the 20th century, produce warehouses, mills, apple dry houses, a malt house, lumberyards and icehouses lined the banks of the canal within the village. Despite the widening of the canal and business relocations, agribusiness remained an important part of the village's economy until the end of the 20th century.

Erie Canal, Pittsford with Schoen Place on right   *Petronio*

Today, although retail shops and restaurants have replaced the agricultural businesses that once operated here, Schoen Place retains four historically significant groups of buildings. At the east end of the street is the Schoen Brothers Coal and Produce Inc. This complex includes several former houses, barns, sheds and a large coal tower, which has been converted into a restaurant. Next is the Pittsford Flour Mills complex. This includes Pittsford's landmark c. 1927, 110-feet-tall concrete grain elevator and the three-story c. 1880 fourmill. Further east is a group of large barns and warehouses comprising the T. J. Zornow Inc. complex. During most of the 20th-century, this was the site of the northeast's largest wholesalers of red kidney beans. At the east end of the street is the Northfield retail complex, which is a former lumber yard.

Over the last twenty-five years, Schoen Place has been transformed into a popular shopping and recreation destination as a result of water-front improvements and the adaptive reuse of the former agricultural and industrial buildings along the narrow, winding road. Today, it is a busy place with strollers and bikers using the canal path. Visitors can also sit and watch boats or feed the resident ducks, while always being reminded of its agricultural past.

Pittsford village is an area with a rich architectural heritage and will be explored further in Chapter 5. To return to Rochester, turn around and return to the city via North Main Street and East Avenue. To continue a tour of Pittsford village, turn left on North Main Street, to the Port of Pittsford located opposite Schoen Place. Here you will begin the "Pittsford to Honeoye Falls" tour in Chapter 5.

North to the Lake:
Downtown to Charlotte

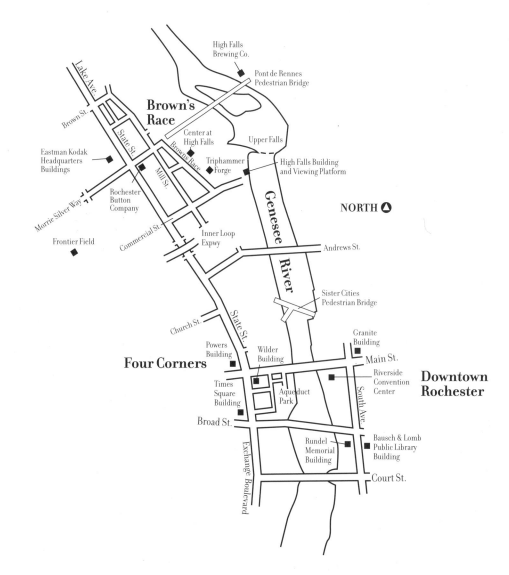

High Falls Brewing Co.

Pont de Rennes Pedestrian Bridge

Brown's Race

Center at High Falls

Upper Falls

Eastman Kodak Headquarters Buildings

Triphammer Forge

High Falls Building and Viewing Platform

Lake Ave.

Brown St.

State St.

Browns Race

Mill St.

NORTH ⏶

Rochester Button Company

Morrie Silver Way

Genesee River

Commercial St.

Inner Loop Expwy

Frontier Field

Andrews St.

Sister Cities Pedestrian Bridge

Church St.

State St.

Granite Building

Powers Building

Wilder Building

Main St.

Four Corners

Downtown Rochester

Riverside Convention Center

Times Square Building

Aqueduct Park

South Ave.

Broad St.

Bausch & Lomb Public Library Building

Exchange Boulevard

Rundel Memorial Building

Court St.

Lake Ontario

Brown's Race

Ontario Beach Park

Charlotte-Genesee Lighthouse and Keeper's Residence Museum

The Secret Sidewalk

NORTH

Stutson St.

Genesee River

Charlotte High School

Turning Point Park

Boxart St.

Lake Avenue

Seneca Park

Riverside Cemetery

Chapel of All Souls, Holy Sepulchre Cemetery, east

Seneca Park Zoo

Route 104

Pedestrian Bridge

Maplewood Park

Holy Sepulchre Cemetery, west

St. Bernard's Seminary

Ridge Rd. W.

Lower Falls Park

Seneca Parkway

Lake Ave.

Maplewood Park Rose Garden

Emerson St.

Jones St.

Jones Square Park

Kodak Office Tower

Edgerton Park

This tour begins at the Four Corners in downtown Rochester, and after making a short loop through the heart of downtown, proceeds north along Lake Avenue, through the historic Edgerton and Maplewood neighborhoods, to Charlotte and ends on the shore of Lake Ontario.

Mileage: Approximately 14 miles

Time: Approximately 1½ hours

~ Open to the Public ~

Rochester Public Library (Central Library)
115 South Avenue
phone 428-7300

The Center at High Falls
60 Browns Race
phone 325-2030

Charlotte-Genesee Lighthouse
and Keeper's Residence Museum
70 Lighthouse Street
phone 621-6179

Edwin Scrantom was only 10 when he walked from the center of Rochester to the harbor at Charlotte. His 1814 journey led him through a dark and wild place. Scrantom wrote, "Three boys started on this journey of seven long miles, over most of which forests hung and walled the road in on both sides ... for variety there were patches of 'corduroy road' that went through swamps that had the interlaced and matted growth of a century where nature had run wild and run mad."

Nature in Rochester in those days included an abundance of rattlesnakes. "They curled up in paths and on the timbers," wrote Elon Huntington Hooker, whose family helped found the early village of Carthage on the east side of the Genesee River. "Men made a living killing rattlesnakes for a bounty of three cents.... Deer, wolves, and wildcats abounded, and bears were numerous." The area also was cursed with a fever resembling malaria, which was dubbed "Genesee Fever."

Today, nearly every inch of property is used for something on this history-rich route from the downtown Four Corners neighborhood north to Lake Ontario. Landmark buildings in the downtown area and in Brown's Race lead to Kodak's earliest buildings (and George Eastman's final resting place), rose gardens, and an impressive array of historic homes and commercial buildings, many proudly detailed with the names of their owners.

The story of how a rattlesnake-infested, inhospitable place became Rochester is a story involving many of the luminaries on this route — industrialists like Eastman Kodak founder George Eastman, whose remains rest in the shadow of Kodak Park; religious figures such as Bishop Bernard McQuaid; and dreamers like the waterfall-jumper Sam Patch.

In the late 18th century, white settlers started streaming into western New York, attracted by lush farmland available for sale following the Revolutionary War. Between 1791 and 1815, at least six settlements were started along the lower Genesee River. These included Charlotte (1791) on Lake Ontario; Hanford Landing, also called King's Landing (1796), near Kodak Park; Carthage on the east bank of the river at Lower Falls (1809); McCrackenville (1815), near Ravine Avenue; Frankfort (1810), near Brown's Race; and the 100-Acre Tract that was sold in 1803 to Colonel Nathaniel Rochester (1752-1831) and two other men from Maryland. The latter settlement, called a shantytown by critics, with its muddy lanes, shacks and cabins, became the village of Rochesterville, which was chartered in 1817.

The steady and unspectacular settlement of Rochesterville changed dramatically, however, when New York state planners decided to build the new canal across the state and through Colonel Nathaniel Rochester's village. With the opening of the Erie Canal in 1825, Rochesterville quickly became America's first "boom town," with settlers, merchants and travelers rushing to the area. By 1834, the population had reached over 12,000, and Rochester was incorporated as a city.

Canal Town

A good place to start this tour is the **Four Corners**, the intersection of Main and State streets and Exchange Boulevard, which was the city's original center, and today remains a hub for banking and government. In 1811, Colonel Nathaniel Rochester surveyed the 100 acres into town lots using a grid system with parallel streets. This very historic area can best be enjoyed on foot. For more information, see *Walking Tours of Downtown Rochester: Images of History*, by the Landmark Society (www.landmarksociety.org). Before viewing the buildings at the Four Corners, take Main Street east toward the river for a tour around one of Rochester's earliest blocks. On the left, at **16 East Main Street**, is the historic **Reynold's Arcade**. One of the earliest buildings in Rochester was constructed at this site — a two-story house erected in 1813 by Abelard Reynolds. In 1828, Reynolds built the five-story Reynold's Arcade in this location. The arcade housed the city's first public library and first central post office, with Abelard Reynolds serving as the city's first postmaster. From 1856 to 1866, the arcade also housed the headquarters of Western Union Telegraph, a hugely successful and important business, founded in Rochester by Hiram Sibley (see also Chapters 1 & 5). The current Reynolds Arcade building is an Art Deco replacement of the previous building and was designed by the architectural firm of Gordon and Kaelber in 1932.

Directly across the street at **25 East Main Street** is the **Talman Building**, where famed abolitionist Frederick Douglass published his anti-slavery newspaper the *North Star* (see sidebar on Frederick Douglass, Chapter 3). To the right, just before the Main Street Bridge, is **Aqueduct Park** and a cluster of late-19th- and early-20th-century industrial buildings. Resting on top of one of the buildings is the landmark statue of Mercury, created in 1881, which first adorned the roof of the former Kimball Tobacco Factory to the south.

Perhaps nothing has changed as much in Rochester's modern era as the Main Street Bridge. The current **Main Street Bridge**, built in 1857, replaced three previous bridges including one made of wood. The earlier bridges fell down or fell apart due to the challenge of crossing the mighty Genesee River, with its ice flows in winter and churning water in spring. For decades, beginning in the 1850s, commercial buildings lined this limestone bridge, obscuring the river. In the 1960s, these buildings were razed, opening up views of the Genesee. The bridge's distinctive guard rail, made of interlaced steel, was designed by Rochester artist Albert Paley, and was provided in 1989 as a gift to the city by Bausch and Lomb Inc.

As you cross the Main Street Bridge, look right at the **Broad Street Bridge**. The lower part of this bridge was considered an engineering marvel when it was constructed in 1842 as the Erie Canal aqueduct, designed to carry canal waters over the Genesee River. The aqueduct, made of Onondaga limestone, was the only one on the Erie Canal to support a trough of water as well as a towpath over a river. The aqueduct, with its seven distinctive arches, is actually the original and lower part of the bridge. The arches were designed to withstand pounding water and ice flows, enabling the passage of water to occur without causing damage to the bridge. The structure replaced a porous sandstone aqueduct built in 1823. After the canal was rerouted in 1920, a second tier was added and paved over for vehicles. Rochester's now defunct subway system used the canal bed from the 1920s until 1956.

After crossing over the bridge, the large building on the right at **123 East Main Street** is the **Riverside Convention Center**, designed by James Stewart Polshek and Partners of New York City, and built in 1982-85. Polshek served as dean of Columbia University's School of Architecture and Planning while working on the convention center.

Before turning right onto South Avenue, look left to the far corner at the tall, cream-colored brick and granite building, called the **Granite Building, 130 East Main Street**. Designed by J. Foster Warner (see sidebar on Andrew J. and J. Foster Warner), it is Rochester's best surviving example of the Beaux Arts style of architecture and features monumental Corinthian columns, arcaded windows and terra cotta details. The 12-story commercial structure was constructed in 1893-94 for the Sibley, Lindsay and Curr Company's retail store and office. A fire in 1904, often called the worst in the city's history, destroyed the entire block, leaving only this building's hollow shell. Sibley's relocated, and the interior of the Granite Building was rebuilt for office and commercial use.

Times Square Building   *Padelt*

Before turning right onto Broad Street, notice the two Rochester Public Library buildings facing each other on the far corners of South Avenue and Broad Streets. On the left side is the central library's **Bausch & Lomb Public Library Building**, designed by William Rawn of Boston and Robert Healey of Rochester, and completed in 1997.

On the right side, at **115 South Avenue**, is the **Rundel Memorial Building** of the Rochester Public Library, a limestone and granite building designed in the Modernistic style by architects Gordon and Kaelber in 1936. Morton Rundel, whose bequest financed the building, was an artist and frame-store owner who amassed more than a million dollars buying Kodak stock in his second cousin George Eastman's business. The library site on the riverbank is unique. It is constructed over an overflow from a former millrace. Arches within the structure allow water to pour back into the river.

As you cross over the Broad Street Bridge, you get another view of the statue of Mercury on the right. Across the street, on the corner, the **Blue Cross Arena at the War Memorial** (1953-55 and 1999), at **1 War Memorial Square**, is on the site of the Kimball Tobacco Factory.

After crossing the Broad Street Bridge, slow down before taking a right on Exchange Boulevard, where there are a number of noteworthy buildings. The Neoclassical **Gannett Building**, on the opposite far corner at **55 Exchange Boulevard**, was built in 1927-28 as headquarters for the *Times-Union* newspaper, now part of the Gannett Company, which has become one of the largest newspaper chains in the country.

Turning onto Exchange Boulevard, the next building on the left is the **Times Square Building**, at **45 Exchange Boulevard**, an Art Deco monument, known for its graceful, winged roof ornament. It was designed by the New York City firm of Voorhees, Gmelin and Walker, with Rochester architect Carl Ade. Built by the Genesee Valley Trust Company, the building's cornerstone was laid on what may have been the most dismal banking day in U.S. history – October 29, 1929, the day the stock market crash launched the Great Depression.

Approaching the Four Corners, the **Wilder Building** is on your right at **8 Exchange Boulevard** at the southeast corner of Main Street. With its rusticated stonework on the first floor and its arched windows and decorative turrets,

Wilder Building

this is the foremost example of Richardsonian Romanesque commercial architecture in Rochester. Constructed in 1888 for Samuel Wilder, a prominent banker and real estate developer, the Wilder Building was designed by Rochester architects Andrew J. Warner and William Brockett. Briefly, it was the tallest building in Rochester,

Across Main Street and on your left is the **Powers Building**. Constructed for local business-man Daniel Powers at **16 West Main Street**, it had a longer reign as the largest and tallest building in the city. This was partly because Powers, to fend off challengers, kept expanding this elaborate Second Empire-style building with new additions. Built in 1869 as a five-story building with a single mansard roof, the building expanded upwards with two more mansard roofs (1880 & 1888), and a tower addition, which went from two stories in 1874 to five stories in 1891. It also was the work of local architect Andrew J. Warner.

Size was not the Powers Building's only distinc-tion; it also had one of the earliest elevators in the United States. In addition, Powers boasted that this stone-and-cast-iron building was fireproof. The interior of the building is a textbook example of cast-iron construction, and features a large,

Powers Building detail   *Petronio*

Andrew J. and J. Foster Warner

The architectural legacy of Andrew J. Warner (1833-1910) and his son J. Foster Warner (1859-1937) spans 90 years and includes many of Rochester's most noted landmarks built between 1847 and 1937.

The Warners' collective genius was responsible for downtown Rochester's most important buildings, including the Powers Building, Wilder Building, Granite Building, former Sibley's building, old City Hall, the Rochester Free Academy, Monroe County Office Building, the former Rochester Savings Bank, and others.

The father and son also designed some of the city's most prominent churches, including Downtown Presbyterian Church, Central Church of Christ (formerly the First Presbyterian Church), and Our Lady of Victory Church. Among their important educational buildings are the Rochester Free Academy (now the Academy Building), East High (now East Court Apartments), and West High School (now Wilson Magnet High School).

While their residential work is found in cities and villages throughout western New York, they were perhaps most prolific in Rochester in the East Avenue Preservation District. J. Foster Warner was involved in the design or alterations of at least 15 houses in this neighborhood, the most notable of which were the Soule House and the George Eastman House.

The parade of styles embraced by the Warners included the Romanesque Revival, High Victorian Gothic, Second Empire, Stick Style, Queen Anne, Beaux-Arts Classicism, Second Renaissance Revival, Georgian Revival, Neoclassical Revival, and Commercial style. Betsy Brayer wrote in the 1984 exhibit catalog, *The Warner Legacy in Western New York*, "While many architects became known as exponents on one style or another, few weathered the fickle changes in taste as the Warners did for half a century each."

open, cast-iron staircase. It housed the city's first art gallery, which closed in 1897.

Next door, at **35 State Street**, is the Classical Revival former bank building, built in 1924. The building features monumental marble fluted Corinthian columns, and a pediment with a wreath framing an eagle with wings spread. The entablature is carved with floral and bird motifs.

While the **Ellwanger and Barry Building** next door at **39-45 State Street** may not look imposing to modern eyes, this eight-story building made of Scotch redstone, brick and iron, seemed massive when it was built in 1887-1888. Constructed by the real estate company formed by the noted nurserymen George Ellwanger and Patrick Barry, who made Rochester famous as "The Flower City" (see Chapter 3), the building was designed by Andrew J. Warner and William Brockett, the team that also designed the Wilder Building.

On the left, just past the Church Street intersection, is an uninterrupted row of 19th-century commercial buildings between **107 and 173 State Street**, which comprise the **State Street National Register Historic District**. Developed between 1825 and 1900, this commercial row was once part of Rochester's 19th-century market area, made up of State Street and nearby Front Street that ran parallel to and between State Street and the river. Continue driving north on State Street past the Inner Loop, then take a right on Platt Street to enter the Brown's Race neighborhood. At the corner of State and Platt Streets (**294-300 State Street**) is the former factory for the Rochester Button Company. The company formerly located in this 1900 building was known as the largest button manufacturer and distributor in the world, importing nuts from Africa, Mexico and South America, which were processed into "vegetable ivory" buttons.

Brown's Race

This area is best seen on foot. There is limited on-street parking. High Falls Garage is accessible from State Street and Mill Street.

Well before there was Kodak film or Xerox copies, water was Rochester's greatest resource. Brown's Race, Rochester's oldest industrial area, was built on the water that tumbled down Brown's Race, a power canal constructed in 1815.

The 1,221-foot-long canal, which ran in the location of the current Browns Race Street, diverted water south of the falls. Water from the race funneled along spillways through the buildings and powered water wheels and turbines for the areas factories and mills. Businesses built fortunes on everything from fire engines to buttons to milled flour, so common here that Rochester was known as the Flour City.

Walk out onto the 1891 Platt Street (now the Pont de Rennes) Bridge to see the spectacular, 96-foot High Falls waterfall. For years, there was no easy public access to the best viewing spot for the falls. In 1982, the 858-foot-long Platt Street Bridge was renovated and renamed the **Pont de Rennes Pedestrian Bridge and Park**, creating a fine public vantage point to see the falls. Standing on the bridge, you can see the spectacular Genesee River gorge, with rock formations of limestone, sandstone, shale and bands of iron ore. The red sandstone in the gorge, known as Medina sandstone, can be found in many older buildings and sidewalks in the area, including the former St. Bernard's Seminary, that we will pass on this tour.

High Falls is renowned as the place that defeated 19th-century daredevil Sam Patch, a professional high-jumper who came to Rochester in 1829 with his trained bear. Patch, who had already jumped Niagara Falls, first made a successful jump of High Falls. He then planned a second jump, which attracted spectators from throughout New York and Canada. Before leaping, he said: "Napoleon was a great general but he couldn't jump the Genesee Falls … I can do it and I will." But he couldn't — and he jumped to his death on Friday, November 13, 1829, to the horror of the approximately 8,000 men, women and children watching.

Brown's Race is Rochester's oldest industrial area. During the early 19th century, there were dozens of mill buildings perched on the edge of the gorge to the right of the falls, which helped make Rochester the flour capital of the world. Most of the existing buildings in the Brown's Race area date to the late 19th century and will be seen later on the tour.

Across the river on the east bank is the **High Falls Brewing Company** (formerly Genesee Brewing Company, established in 1878), the only large brewery left from the days when Rochester was a center for breweries. These included impressive operations such as the Bartholomay Brewery Company, whose remaining buildings are now part of High Falls Brewing. Founded in 1875, Bartholomay Brewery owned a six-acre complex with 15 buildings, 165 refrigerator cars to ship beer by train, and 75 horse-drawn wagons for local delivery.

Just north of the Pont-de-Rennes Bridge, looking away from downtown and High Falls, is the **Bausch Memorial Bridge**, a steel cantilever construction bridge which stretches 945 feet across the gorge and 105 feet above the river. The bridge is named after German immigrants John Jacob Bausch (1830-1926) and Captain Henry Lomb (1825-1908), founders of Bausch and Lomb, the world-renowned optics company. Bausch was an eyeglass salesman who ground the first American-made lenses because he was not satisfied with the European lenses he sold in his eyeglass shop. Lomb invested early in the business as Bausch's partner. In 1885 Lomb, a skilled European craftsman, helped found the Mechanics Institute – precursor to Rochester Institute of Technology (see Chapter 3) – to train a new generation of technical workers.

The **Bausch and Lomb factories** were located at **635 St. Paul Street** until the early 1970s, when the company moved its manufacturing plant to 1400 North Goodman Street. Bronze tablets on the west side of Bausch Bridge honor Bausch, and a 48-foot high, Art Deco black granite obelisk pays tribute to Lomb on the St. Paul Boulevard side of the bridge at Bausch Street.

On the northwest bank of the river gorge is **Beebee Station** of the Rochester Gas and Electric Company. In 1892, one of the company's predecessors established a combined steam and hydroelectric plant here. Although Beebee Station produces electricity from coal, gas and oil, R G & E still uses Brown's Race for hydroelectric power.

As you leave the Pont-de-Rennes, you pass, on the right, the **Phoenix Mill Building**, at **104 Platt Street**. Built in 1819, this building is distinguished by unusual twelve-light, single-sash windows and three well-worn stone walls. The brick south wall was constructed after a large portion of the building was removed to make way for the 1891 Platt Street Bridge.

Now you can return to the High Falls historic area to view other notable buildings. The area,

now a National and State District and a City
Preservation District, has seen a renaissance
in recent years.

Around the corner from Platt Street is **The
Center at High Falls**, at **74-78 Browns Race**.
An urban cultural park exhibit center, the building
is open to the public and interprets Rochester
history, particularly as it relates to the High Falls
area. The brick, High Victorian Gothic building
was designed by Andrew J. Warner, with Gaines-
ville sandstone trim and an unusual cast-iron
cornice. Formerly the Rochester Water Works,
the structure was constructed in 1873 to provide
high-pressure water for downtown fire fighting.
It also generated hydraulic power for elevators,
including those in the Powers Building.

You may continue walking or return to your
car to view the rest of the area. From your car,
turn right from Platt Street onto Mill Street. On
your left, is a series of commercial 19th-century
buildings, starting with **222-230 Mill Street**.
Originally a barrel factory, the building was
constructed in 1851 and modified in the 1870s.
You can see loading doors, which had a hoist
and pulley on each floor, and a projecting
cornice with corbeled frieze.

Rochester Water Works, Brown's Race   *Petronio*

Next, on the left, at **208 Mill Street**, is the 1826 stone **Selye Fire Engine Company Building**. Notice the loading doors on each floor and the hoist and pulley on the top. The company built Rochester's first fire engines and supplied federal fortifications and other cities across the state.

Turn left on Commercial Street. On the right, at **61 Commercial Street**, is a nicely renovated **New York Railway Company power house**, built in the 1890s. Opposite, at **Nos. 60-64**, is a former window sash industrial building, constructed in 1880. At the end of the street is the large brick Gorsline Building, built in 1888 as a shoe factory. Stonework on the lower portion shows evidence of earlier buildings. Rochester was one of the world's shoe capitals, with 64 shoe factories listed in 1898. In 2000, the building was transformed into the **High Falls Building**. One third of the derelict structure was renovated for offices and another section was demolished. With the remaining property, the City of Rochester created a terrace for viewing the gorge and the spillway pit that once powered the factory.

Turn left onto Browns Race and look down and right at the only exposed portion of the original 1815 raceway. Farther down, on the right at the edge of the gorge, is the site of the former **Triphammer Forge**. The building was constructed in 1816 and used as a tool factory. It burned in 1977, and when the rubble was cleared, a long-forgotten basement room was uncovered that housed the building's massive 25-foot water wheel, constructed of wood and iron. Now a unique archaeological park, the Triphammer Forge site provides a good view of one of the layers of history in Brown's Race.

To continue the tour, turn left on Furnace Street, right on Mill Street, left on Platt Street, and then right onto State Street.

Kodak Country

With its characteristic block letters spelling "Kodak" at the base of the roof, there's no mistaking the **Kodak Office Tower** at **343 State Street**, which looms over the Brown's Race Historic District. The building is a bricks-and-mortar reminder of Eastman Kodak Company's powerful influence on Rochester. Constructed in stages, the building's first 16 stories were built in 1914. Three more floors, a cupola and a roof were added in 1930.

George Eastman's invention of a practical dry plate for photographers was the first of many Kodak discoveries that made photography easier for professionals and more accessible to the public. Eastman, who dropped out of school at age 13, launched his first factory in a third-floor loft at 343 State Street. The first Kodak building at this location was a four-story office building opened in 1882 to house Eastman's Dry Plate and Film Company.

Directly across from the Kodak offices, on the right, is a row of five three-story brick commercial buildings, dating from the 1840s and '50s. Designed in the Federal style, these buildings belonged to the early settlement of Frankfort village, established in 1810 by the Brown brothers. These buildings housed stores and businesses serving the Brown's Race area.

At the intersection with Lyell Avenue, State Street becomes Lake Avenue. The words "Lake Avenue" once signaled a world of affluence and grandeur. Lake Avenue in the late 1800s rivaled East Avenue as a home for Rochester's rich and powerful. Traces of Lake Avenue's glamorous past can be found up and down the avenue, in gracious homes and commercial buildings tucked primly between fast food restaurants, car washes and the diverse commercial mix that is the avenue today. Influential residents in the late-19th century included Henry Strong, the first president of Eastman Dry Plate and Film Company; Edmund F. Woodbury, president of the Woodbury Whip Company; and his son John C. Woodbury, father of Margaret Woodbury Strong, whose lifelong collection is the heart of the Strong Museum.

As stable but less elegant residential neighborhoods grew up around Lake Avenue in the early 1900s, the avenue lost its allure for the affluent. Henry Strong moved to East Avenue in 1902, and many others followed, fleeing a street that had become less exclusive with the influx of trolleys, Kodak workers, and new immigrants. As the avenue changed, evidence of these elite residents was frequently obliterated in the dust and debris of razed homes and new construction, much of it commercial.

All that was in the future when, in 1869, Walter Duffy moved his Duffy Distilleries (established 1847) to the corner of White Street. In 1904, at **81 Lake Avenue**, the Rochester Distilling Company built this attractive brick building, notable for its decorative terra cotta detailing above the second floor. The building has been renovated after more than 70 years as Judge's Ford Motor Corporation, which succeeded the distillery in the 1920s.

Several mid-to-late-19th-century residences are located in this section of Lake Avenue, though you may have to look carefully to find some of them. On the left, at the corner of Lake and Ambrose streets, is **143-145 Lake Avenue**, an 1872 brick Italianate residence, featuring a prominent wood cornice with scroll-sawn brackets. This was the home of Edmund F. Woodbury and later his son John C. Woodbury, father of Margaret Woodbury Strong, who continued to reside here until 1923.

Next to Ambrose Street is Jones Street. Turn left onto Jones Street for a brief tour of one of the oldest public squares in the city, **Jones Square Park**. At the end of Jones Street, turn right onto Plymouth Avenue. Dating from the 1830s as a planned urban green space, the seven-acre park was redesigned by Frederick Law Olmsted at the turn of the 20th century. (See sidebar on Frederick Law Olmsted, Chapter 2.) Now drive completely around the park, making left turns and returning to Plymouth Avenue. A variety of mid-to-late-19th-century houses, vernacular in style, cluster around the park.

At the corner of Jones and Plymouth avenues, at **43 Jones Avenue**, is the **First Assembly Church of God**, a city-designated landmark. Built in 1880-81 as Trinity Episcopal Church, this edifice was designed in the High Victorian Gothic style by Andrew J. Warner. The handsome edifice is constructed of gray stone with Medina sandstone trim, with a tall slate-shingled tower that is a visual landmark in the neighborhood.

To return to Lake Avenue, turn right on Plymouth, and left on Ambrose. Turn left onto Lake Avenue.

As Lake Avenue changed, so too, did the Edgerton neighborhood which grew up to the west of the avenue. Stretching from Lyell Avenue at the south to Driving Park Avenue at the north, for years this historic neighborhood was central to Rochester's cultural and recreational life. At its heart was Edgerton Park, which was the cradle of many of Rochester's cultural institutions and was promoted as the symbol of a young and growing metropolitan area.

For a brief detour, turn left onto Phelps Avenue, which leads to **Edgerton Park**. Turn right onto Backus Street and pause briefly here. The park (on the left) originally was the site of a state reform school for juvenile delinquents that opened in 1849. The large brick building with arched windows, classical details and stone trim is the only surviving building from the school. Built in the 1890s as the chapel, it later became an assembly hall, and is now a city-owned recreation center. The stone pillars are remnants of the once-solid school fence.

In 1911, the city acquired the 42-acre property and named it Exposition Park. Among its attractions were a zoo, an aquarium, industrial exhibition buildings, and more. Mayor Hiram Edgerton encouraged the addition of cultural services, and the Rochester Historical Society, as well as the forerunners of the Rochester Museum & Science Center, the Memorial Art Gallery, and the Rochester Public Library were located here. After Mayor Edgerton's death, the park was renamed in his honor in 1922 and was the site of athletic events, including horse shows, rodeos, and basketball tournaments until the War Memorial was erected in the 1950s.

Proceed on Backus Street and turn right on Emerson Street, which jogs slightly at Fulton Avenue before returning to Lake Avenue. Turn left onto Lake Avenue.

You can easily spot the distinctive Richardsonian Romanesque stone and brick apartment buildings on the right at **512-514 Lake Avenue** by their radiating arched entries and stone trim. Built in 1889-1890, they are among the oldest apartment dwellings on the avenue.

Here the building stock changes from residential dwellings to commercial and apartment structures, many dating from the late-19th and early-20th centuries. These buildings, with their careful attention to detail, contrast with many of today's apartment buildings and box-like commercial structures. The group of commercial buildings around the intersection of Ravine Avenue is located near the early-19th-century trade and mill settlement of McCrackenville. Now part of the Edgerton neighborhood, the area reflects the urban development that began here in the second half of the 19th century.

On the right, at the northeast corner of Lake and Ravine avenues, is the **Straub's Block**, a striking commercial building at **596-604 Lake Avenue**. Erected in 1874, it was originally a grocery store that also sold beer and animal feed. This finely detailed, three-story building features decorative brick and pressed-metal cornice, patterned brickwork, and a cast-iron storefront.

Abutting the Straub's Block is the brick-and-cast-stone commercial and apartment building at **606-614 Lake Avenue**, which also is eclectic and finely detailed. Built in 1915-16, the building features a sculpted, pressed-metal cornice of classical elements, and a handsome, round-arched cast-stone center entrance surround bearing a large, scrolled keystone.

Across the street, at **601 Lake Avenue**, is a unique example of an early Lake Avenue apartment building. Built in 1888 and designed in the Chateauesque style, it is distinguished by the round turret at the south end, as well as the two-story bay windows and shingled mansard roof.

At the southwest corner of Glendale Park (on the left), at **633-639 Lake Avenue**, is the three-story **Ferner Building**, an interesting commercial brick building constructed in 1891 for grocer John Ferner. Notice the building's center pediment with the name "Ferner," and the split date 1891 molded in the flanking archways above the third-floor windows.

From Races to Roses

Proceed north on Lake Avenue to Driving Park Avenue and Maplewood Park's Rose Garden. The garden marks the beginning of the Maplewood neighborhood, which includes a National Register Historic District with an abundance of gracious homes, and parkland stretching north to Holy Sepulchre and Riverside cemeteries. Driving Park Avenue derives its name from a nationally known racetrack, Rochester Driving Park, which was in operation from 1874 to 1895, and was located just north of the avenue. The grounds hosted horse races (a world record was set there by the trotter Maud S. in 1881), circuses, bicycle races, and shows such as Buffalo Bill's Wild West Show.

Turn right onto Driving Park Avenue and left into the parking lot of **Maplewood Park**. Maplewood Park originally was created as part of Seneca Park, which was Frederick Law Olmsted's plan to establish a linear park straddling the river gorge (see sidebars on Seneca Park and Frederick Law Olmsted).

The original Driving Park Bridge, built in 1893 and dedicated as Seneca Park Bridge, connected both sides. Later land acquisitions included the "Maple Grove," a German beer garden resort owned by the George Ellwanger family (see Chapter 3), and extended the park to 144 acres. Since the early 1900s, the park has been used for public recreational activities, from concerts, to skating, to golf.

A rose garden was first planted here in the 1920s. In 1951 the **Maplewood Park Rose Garden** was dedicated and opened to the public through a cooperative effort between the city of Rochester and the Rochester Rose Society. The garden boasts over 250 varieties of roses, including ancient strains (the Austrian Copper is an orange mutant of a rose first discovered in 1590), as well as double roses, climbing roses, miniature roses, and new hybrids being tested. If you wish, take the trail to the **Lower Falls Park**, located nearby.

While the Genesee River is often overlooked by contemporary travelers driving up Lake Avenue, in the late 19th century, the river was celebrated for its beauty. A luxurious resort called the Glen House opened in 1870 at the bottom of the gorge near the Lower Falls. Travelers reached the resort by steamboat from Charlotte, or by a hydraulic elevator, which operated on the west side of the gorge. The hotel was destroyed by fire in 1894, and only the concrete base of the hydraulic elevator remains as a reminder of this once-popular river resort.

Leaving the parking lot, look across the street to the **Maplewood YMCA**, at **25 Driving Park Avenue**. A neighborhood landmark since its construction in 1916, it was designed by Rochester architect Claude Bragdon (see sidebar, Chapter 3). The building exhibits many typical Bragdon elements, including muted brown and patterned brick and glazed terra cotta ornamentation. The bold entrance features marble columns and polychrome tile decoration.

Turn right on Lake Avenue and left onto Lake View Park. **Lake View Park** was the area's earliest residential subdivision, laid out in 1872, with

Frederick Law Olmsted and the Rochester Park System

The Rochester Park System, including Highland, Genesee Valley, and Seneca parks, was designed in the final creative years of Frederick Law Olmsted (1822-1903), who is acclaimed as America's greatest landscape architect and father of the profession.

Olmsted had explored many careers before becoming a parks designer. He was a scientific farmer, a journalist, and a publisher before winning the design competition in 1857 with Calvert Vaux to create Central Park in New York City. America's first urban park, Central Park served as a model for many cities throughout the country. Olmsted's firm and the subsequent firm, Olmsted Brothers, established in 1898 by his son Frederick Law Olmsted, Jr. and stepson, John C. Olmsted, ultimately gained credit for establishing landscape architecture as a profession.

Olmsted's parks are known for their artful use of three natural elements: turf (grass areas), water and woods. He utilized and emphasized existing topography of rivers, gorges, and hills – all components of Rochester's Olmsted parks. His parks provided city dwellers with the opportunity to enjoy natural beauty and partake in recreational activities.

Rochester's park system, constructed between the late 1880s and 1916, encompassed not only the three major parks, but also 11 small parks and squares. In 1899, city parklands totaled 652 acres.

While Olmsted lived until 1903, he retired from active work in 1895. The firm owned by the Olmsted Brothers continued to advise the city on work on the park system until 1916. Cobbs Hill Reservoir was enlarged from a gift of 15 acres from George Eastman in 1904. Durand Eastman Park was created after Henry Durand and George Eastman donated 484 acres in 1908.

Although many cities have an Olmsted park, Rochester is one of only six American cities (including Boston, Buffalo, Brooklyn, Chicago, and Louisville) with park systems designed by Frederick Law Olmsted. Rochester has changed dramatically since Olmsted's day, but his vision of parkland providing a respite from city life has endured.

a large central green space. Twenty years earlier, the hillside property was the home of the Lake View Water Cure, which offered a homeopathic treatment to visitors. In the 1890s, the city commissioned the Olmsted firm to prepare plans for landscape improvements of the central mall. Drive around the mall to enjoy this attractive street and the several notable late-19th-century homes built in the Stick style (**No. 30**), Queen Anne style (**No. 53**), and Shingle style (**No. 45**).

Returning to Lake Avenue, look left at the corner at the **Nazareth Academy** complex. Then, turn left onto Lake Avenue and pull over to study the attractive brick-and-slate shingle former carriage house at **977 Lake Avenue**. Built in 1890, the carriage house was originally part of the former Lewis Selye estate, which included a massive Queen Anne residence known as the "Glass House." The main brick school building was built in 1915 for the Academy, a secondary school for girls, which opened in 1916.

Continuing on Lake Avenue, note on the right the sumptuous red brick, Colonial Revival residence at **1040 Lake Avenue**, built in 1907 for John K. Hunt, a paper box manufacturer. Designed by local architects Crandall & Strobel,

the house features a prominent, pedimented portico, with Corinthian columns and classical ornamentation.

Proceed north to **Seneca Parkway** to see another residential neighborhood that is architecturally rich. Turn left onto the parkway; drive as far as you wish to enjoy this splendid collection of early-20th-century styles of domestic architecture, including Colonial Revival, Tudor Revival, Mission and Craftsman. Seneca Parkway was laid out in accordance with the vision of a parkway system encircling the city, developed by Frederick Law Olmsted, Sr. and Co. Seneca Parkway is the development in which this concept was partially realized. During the decades of the 1910s and '20s, a time of growth and prosperity in the city, middle- and upper-middle-class houses were built on large lots here and in other nearby developments.

Return to Lake Avenue, turn left and proceed one block north. On the left is the striking, Second Empire **Vanderbeck House** at **No. 1295**, one of the oldest and most prominent residences on the avenue. The house presided over a 200-acre farm parcel when it was built in 1874 for the well-established businessman Andrew

Lower Falls of the Genesee River   *Petronio*

Vanderbeck. The three-story brick house has a slate mansard roof, punctuated by round-arched windows that are highlighted with heavy moldings and dentil trim. Four years after the house was built, Vanderbeck died in a carriage accident, leaving his wife and two children.

Continuing on Lake Avenue, there is a dramatic change in scenery with the first of many massive **Kodak Park** buildings as Lake Avenue crosses busy **Route 104** (**Ridge Road**). In 1891, four buildings were constructed on the original 16-acre park, so named for its landscaped, park-like appearance. Among the important manufacturing processes first developed here was the making of commercial transparent roll film used in motion pictures.

George Eastman's ashes rest in a bronze urn at the Eastman Memorial, a monument set within a circular plaza of Georgian rose marble and surrounded by weeping beech trees, which can be seen on the left in front of Kodak Park.

Just north of and across from the factory buildings is a street sign, Hanford Landing Road. At the corner of Maplewood Drive is a small, treed park, with a historical marker for King's Landing.

Seneca Park

A century ago, Frederick Law Olmsted designed Seneca Park, a 212-acre scenic reservation on both sides of the Genesee River. The park is one of three major parks in the Rochester Park System designed by Olmsted. The other two are Highland and Genesee Valley (see Chapter 3). Seneca Park was designed as a linear park, stretching like a ribbon along both sides of the Genesee River, to preserve and enhance the picturesque wilderness of the river gorge.

Olmsted's design offered carriage drives and extensive pathways that gave the visitor spectacular vistas of the river and gorge. The emphasis on native trees and horticultural specimen stock made the park a distinctive rustic wilderness. The man-made, five-acre Trout Pond was designed as a water feature in lower Seneca Park and was used for boating, ice-skating, and fishing. Visitors can still enjoy the lake and the wooded trails along the edge of the gorge.

The original plans called for greater development of trails and boat landings within the park than were eventually created. The Carthage settlement landing on the east side provided safe access to the river edge and to a boat livery. Olmsted designed other areas for sheltered boat landings, as well as a walking path that led to and along the edge of the river. However, the city was unable to purchase land from the Rochester School for the Deaf, and portions of the planned carriage drive were never built.

Seneca Park has been changed over the years. The **Seneca Park Zoo**, which is constructed on parkland, began as a collection of animals housed in small cages set out among the trees. An aviary was built in 1897 near Trout Lake. The present menagerie building was erected on the site in 1931. The west side of Seneca Park was re-established as Maplewood Park in 1904. Other sections of the parkland on both sides of the river also have been used for non-park purposes, including senior citizen housing and a sewage disposal plant.

Olmsted's original design has changed, except in the lower park, which remains true to the original design intent. Native deer and other wildlife remain, and the park continues to offer a natural, 'wild' place at the edge of the Genesee River for the enjoyment of Rochester's citizens.

In 1796, Gideon King, Elijah Kent and Zadock Granger established a settlement here with a landing on the river. Abram Hanford built the Old Hanford Tavern in 1809. DeWitt Clinton stopped here in 1810 for rest and refreshment while on an exploratory tour with other members of the state Canal Commission.

The Final Rest

Beyond Kodak Park, the terrain changes again, opening up to greenery and trees for the first time on the route. The landscape serves as a backdrop to a former seminary and shades the graves of the dead in the gracious Holy Sepulchre and Riverside cemeteries.

The Victorian Gothic **St. Bernard's Seminary** on the right, at **2260 Lake Avenue**, was one of the last projects of Bishop Bernard J. McQuaid (1823-1909), the first bishop of the Catholic Diocese of Rochester. Built from 1891-1908, the seminary trained 2,900 priests before closing in 1981. Though he was in his late 60s during its beginning construction, the Bishop reportedly inspected the progress of work on the seminary daily, sometimes climbing the scaffolding to get a closer look. St. Bernard's, with its striking red

St. Bernard's Seminary   *Petronio*

Medina stone details, was designed by Andrew J. Warner on a spectacular site high above the Genesee gorge that McQuaid adored. A 1940 account said the bishop would walk the high banks of the river for hours, "using only matches for light so as not to attract attention." In 1996 the building was converted to housing for senior citizens.

Just past St. Bernard's, the sprawling, 320-acre **Holy Sepulchre Cemetery** begins. Turn right through the main entrance gate and drive around the circle, stopping in front of **The Chapel of All Souls**. When the cemetery opened in 1871, all local Catholic burials were required to take place here. The order remained until 1960, making this the final resting place for generations of Catholics, including Patrick Barry, the horticulturist co-founder of Ellwanger and Barry; Al Sigl, the broadcaster and humanitarian; and Catherine DeValera Wheelwright, mother of Eamon DeValera, the president of Ireland. Early rules in the cemetery, such as the limit of 12 carriages per funeral, were intended "to avoid worldly show." But the graveyard, with its extensive plantings and elaborate headstones, offers worldly pleasures of its own, which you can experience on foot or from your car.

Chapel of All Souls, Holy Sepulchre Cemetery   *Petronio*

The Chapel of All Souls, designed by Andrew J. Warner in 1875, is an English Gothic-style chapel constructed of mottled Medina sandstone. In 1886, the crenellated and turreted freestanding tower was added. The tower was planned to house a water system for the cemetery, as well as a bell. Neither the water system nor the bell was installed until the summer of 2000, when cemetery officials hung a bell that came from the vacated chapel at the correctional facility in Sonyea, New York. The inscription on the bell reads: "In memory of Rt. Rev. B. J. McQuaid, First Bishop of Rochester, 1868 - 1909, A.D. 1909."

Return to Lake Avenue and turn right. Just north of Holy Sepulchre is **Riverside Cemetery**, on the right at **2650 Lake Avenue**, which opened in 1892 and is now owned by the City of Rochester. W. W. Parce, who worked in the Olmsted firm, was the cemetery's landscape architect and first superintendent. The handsome gatehouse and superintendent's residence were built in 1891. The Gleason family, including Kate Gleason, and the Edmund Lyon family (see Chapter 1) are among the prominent people buried here.

Farther along Lake Avenue, behind some residential streets, is **Turning Point Park**. The park can be reached by taking a right turn onto Boxart Street, just before the railroad bridge, and following the road to the end. Created in 1977, the park highlights the spectacular scenery of the lower Genesee gorge – a place to hike, canoe, and view waterfalls and bird life. Yet, as recently as the 1950s, the area was best known as the takeoff point where coal was delivered by rail and loaded onto cargo ships for Canada.

Coney Island of the West

Continuing north, you enter the Charlotte neighborhood of the city of Rochester, once an independent village built around Lake Ontario. Though Charlotte became part of the city in 1915, the expanded residential and commercial neighborhood has maintained its village character.

The large, tan brick school on the right, at **3330 Lake Avenue**, is the **Abelard Reynolds School No. 42**, named after the Rochester pioneer who established the Reynolds Arcade on Main Street that you saw earlier on this tour.

Built in 1927, the school exhibits Romanesque and Byzantine elements. The cast-stone entrance is embellished with Byzantine capitals and two large cast-stone owls.

Farther north, on the right, we pass a long stone wall. This wall once surrounded the late-19th-century estate of Arthur G. Yates, owner of the Yates Coal Company, the Rochester-Pittsburgh Coal Company, and the Buffalo, Rochester, and Pittsburgh Railroad. His property stretched down to the west bank of the Genesee River, where his docks were located for shipping coal to Canada. Later, these were superceded by the coal trestle at Turning Point Park.

Another school worth a close look is the former **Charlotte High School**, now a middle school, on the left at **4115 Lake Avenue**. Built in 1931-33, this brick-and-cast-stone building is one of the most important Art Deco-style structures in the city. The enormous, octagonal tower, with eight large projecting rectangular buttresses, is unique, as are the ornate carved-stone plaques, which depict scenes of new and old immigrants and their ships. Notice, too, that the octagonal stone lampposts flanking the entrance are fashioned

to look like abstract lighthouses. Both schools were designed by Francis R. Sherer, who was chief architect for the state Board of Education.

Charlotte is graced with several fine churches. At **4352 Lake Avenue**, on the right, is the former **St. George's Episcopal Church**. The oldest section, built in 1891, is contained in the large gable end, which has a recessed, pointed arch embellished with a large, round bas-relief panel of St. George slaying the dragon.

Visible from a distance is the very tall, square tower of **Holy Cross Church**, located on the right at **4490 Lake Avenue**. Turn right into the large parking lot just past the church. Designed by Rochester architect Andrew J. Warner (see sidebar, Chapter 2), the Gothic structure was constructed in 1881 of Medina sandstone. The tower, which has a more modern appearance, was extended to its present height in 1894.

This is a good place to view the **Charlotte-Genesee Lighthouse and Keeper's Residence Museum**, which is open to the public. It was on this site that Charlotte's first white settler, farmer William Hincher, built a home for his wife and seven children in 1791. In 1805, the federal

View from the Secret Sidewalk   *Petronio*

government, under President Thomas Jefferson, established the port of Charlotte. Hincher's wife deeded the lakeshore property to the government, and in 1822, the handsome 40-foot stone tower was built, the first lighthouse erected on the shores of Lake Ontario. A winding wrought-iron staircase leads up to the restored Fresnel lens, the original of which was visible for 20 miles. The present brick keeper's house was built in 1863.

Continue north on Lake Avenue and turn into the beach parking lot on the right. Within a few short decades, Charlotte was transformed from a wilderness outpost to a community best known for its beaches, gambling, and amusement park entertainment. Although there were visitors to the beach in earlier years, the area took off as a resort in 1874, when the New York Central Railroad built tracks to **Ontario Beach Park**. Later, electric trolleys followed suit, providing direct service from downtown. Hotels and pavilions were constructed, and permanent amusements, including a roller coaster and a carousel, were built.

A May 31, 1907, account from the *Democrat and Chronicle* reported on a day at the beach: "Ontario Beach Park inside its big high walls has a regular little Coney Island — performing animals, merry-go-rounds, dance halls, goodness only knows what else. Enough to give a small boy a whole day of his idea of what perfect happiness would be .... It was estimated that 40,000 persons saw the sights yesterday and became young again under the influence of popcorn, peanuts and lemonade in assorted flavors." The appeal of the park lessened after the early 1900s, but its lovely bathing beach remained. The beach and its pavilion, complete with gazebos and a boardwalk, have been renovated, and today are a popular summer attraction, as is the 1905 **Denzel Carousel**, a Rochester City Landmark, which was restored in 1984.

Return to Lake Avenue, and at the end, turn left onto Beach Avenue, which leads to a group of attractive homes on the right at the water's edge. The most distinctive is "**Shingleside**," at **476 Beach Avenue**, a large, wood-shingled, gambrel-roofed house designed by Rochester architect Claude Bragdon. Constructed in 1898-99, the house is an eclectic combination of the Shingle- and Colonial Revival-styles. Built for clothing manufacturer Nathan Stein, the house was one of Bragdon's first commissions as an independent architect.

West of Shingleside is the so-called "**Secret Sidewalk**," one of the little-known pleasures in the neighborhood. Public access to the walkway is located between **490-510 Beach Avenue** and continues to **No. 720**. Drivers can park their cars on one of the side streets in the neighborhood. The public walkway follows the shoreline and offers a sweeping view of Lake Ontario, as well as a distinctive view of this waterside neighborhood, complete with well-tended gardens. Walking among the flowers, watching the water of Lake Ontario, strollers can enjoy as quiet and peaceful a slice of city life as one is likely to find anywhere.

Then there is the lake, which retains much of the grandeur that made young Edwin Scrantom "transfixed with wonder" at the end of his seven-mile walk to Charlotte in 1814. Remembering the walk 60 years later, Scrantom could see the sight clearly. "The wind was high, and the white breakers were all along the shore .... Beyond was the rolling commotion of the waves, and way out, as I thought, a hundred miles, the surface of the waters touched the sky."

Downtown Rochester

Old Stone Warehouse

Averill Ave.

Ford Street Bridge

Mt. Hope Ave.

Cypress St.

Ellwanger Garden

Linden St.

Highland Bowl

S. Goodman St.

Robinson Dr.

Colgate Rochester
Divinity School

Genesee River

Lamberton Conservatory

Reservoir Ave.

University
of Rochester

Mt. Hope
Cemetery

Mt. Hope Ave.

Warner
Castle

Elmwood Ave.

Highland Ave.

Genesee Valley Park

Elmwood Ave.

Strong
Memorial
Hospital

Eastman
Dental
Center

South Ave.

NORTH ▲

Moore Drive

Erie Canal

E. River Rd.

Genesee Valley Park

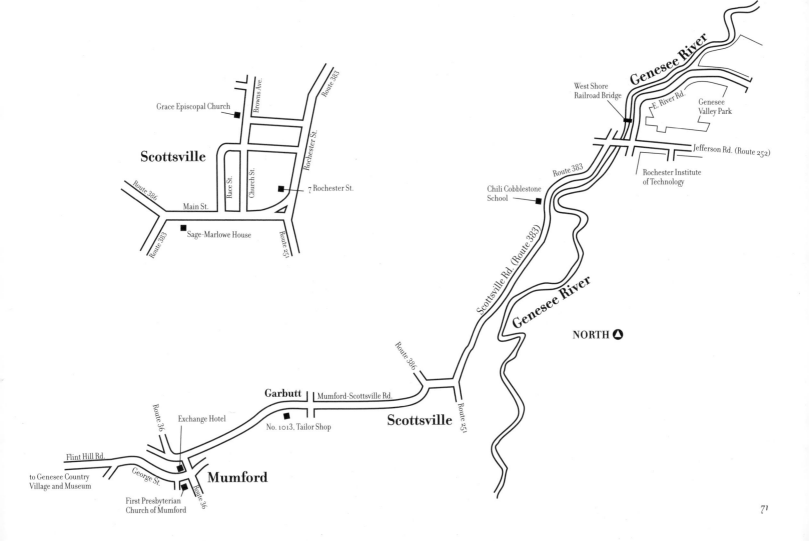

Scottsville

Grace Episcopal Church

Browns Ave.

Route 383

Rochester St.

Race St.

Church St.

Main St.

Route 386

Route 383

7 Rochester St.

Route 251

Sage-Marlowe House

Genesee River

West Shore Railroad Bridge

E. River Rd.

Genesee Valley Park

Jefferson Rd. (Route 252)

Route 383

Rochester Institute of Technology

Chili Cobblestone School

Scottsville Rd. (Route 383)

Genesee River

NORTH

Route 386

Garbutt

Mumford-Scottsville Rd.

Scottsville

Route 251

Route 36

Exchange Hotel

No. 1013, Tailor Shop

Flint Hill Rd.

to Genesee Country Village and Museum

George St.

Mumford

Route 36

First Presbyterian Church of Mumford

This tour begins near downtown Rochester, at the corner of South and Mt. Hope Avenues, and proceeds south and west, alongside the Genesee River, to the village of Scottsville, ending at the Genesee Country Museum in Mumford.

Mileage: Approximately 31 miles, including the optional tour (R.I.T. campus)

Time: Approximately 1½ hours

~ Open to the Public ~

Ellwanger Garden
625 Mt. Hope Avenue, phone 546-7029

Mt. Hope Cemetery
1133 Mt. Hope Avenue, phone 473-2755

Rochester Civic Garden Center/Warner Castle
5 Castle Park, phone 473-5130

Lamberton Conservatory
Reservoir Drive, phone 256-5878

Genesee Country Village & Museum
1410 Flint Hill Road, Mumford, phone 538-6822

Even on the stormiest days

there's a steady stream of cars up and down Mt. Hope Avenue, where this route begins. Looking back 100 years, Mt. Hope was a cobblestone street so quiet it could be used as a sledding hill on a snowy night. Indeed, a 1965 newspaper column by Henry W. Clune described bobsledding down the street with his friend Gaius Moore and others in the early 1900s.

"With 10 or 12 of us astride the long board set on runners ... we careered down Mt. Hope Avenue hill from Reservoir Avenue to Clarissa Street.... All Gaius Moore, steering his bobsled, needed to be concerned about was the Toonerville Trolley, which bobbed and rattled into Mt. Hope Avenue only at rare intervals."

Starting at the northern end of Mt. Hope, our route to Scottsville leads through two parks designed by Frederick Law Olmsted (Highland and Genesee Valley) and two institutions of higher learning (University of Rochester and Rochester Institute of Technology). We travel southwest along both sides of the Genesee River to historic Scottsville and end at the Genesee Country Village and Museum, a recreated historic village.

Even by 1900, the Mt. Hope Avenue that Clune remembered had a rich architectural heritage. We begin at the corner of South and Mt. Hope avenues next to the **Old Stone Warehouse**. This historic intersection once was the location of a bend in the Erie Canal and a now-defunct canal "feeder," which ran parallel to the river and serviced river traffic, connecting it to the Erie Canal. It was a natural spot for the storage of freight awaiting transport.

In the early-to-middle 1800s, the Genesee River was a hectic place with abundant traffic, particularly in spring when water was running high. The river and the Erie Canal were main passageways for grain coming from farmers in Wheatland and other towns outside Rochester. In 1834, there was a 90-foot sternwheeler that carried 300 passengers between Rochester and Geneseo, a trip that took between two and three days. There also were rafts that were 'poled' along the rapid water.

Yet the Genesee was threateningly unpredictable, and likely to flood if conditions were right. Throughout the 19th and early-20th centuries, floods regularly battered downtown Rochester and communities along the river. Rochester's downtown was devastated in 1865 when water flooded the city, rising to six feet at the Four Corners. Logs carried by the river smashed through building walls, and the city was left in darkness when the gas plant was submerged. Two streetcars stopped running on the Main Street Bridge and passengers needed to be evacuated. Once the passengers were removed, the cars traveled downstream and one car toppled over the falls. For days, water was so high that rowboats were the only method of transport through the streets. Completion of the 215-foot Mt. Morris Dam in 1951 dramatically reduced flooding.

On the right, just before turning onto Mt. Hope Avenue from South Avenue, is the Old Stone Warehouse at **1 Mt. Hope Avenue**, the oldest existing commercial structure in Rochester. Built next to the Erie Canal in 1822 and made of red Medina sandstone, the warehouse you see today encompasses the original building and two additions added later. The warehouse had a brief life (about two years) as a major storage facility for freight awaiting transport while the first Erie Canal aqueduct was being built across the Genesee River. After the canal was completed, and the storage and freight business shifted to the west side of the river, the warehouse was abandoned until the 1830s, when the building was used as a foundry for stoves. Later, it served as a malt house and then a warehouse once again. After fire damaged the building in 1975, it appeared slated for demolition until a developer purchased and renovated the city-designated landmark in 1986, returning it to an active life as office space.

Driving south on Mt. Hope Avenue, with the river to the right, the route passes through the edge of the South Wedge neighborhood, which you can see on your left. A quick visit to this historic, pie-shaped residential and commercial neighborhood can be accomplished by taking a left onto Gregory Street (two streets after the second light). Most buildings in the area were constructed in the late 19th century.

Just past the intersection of Ashland Street is the **Marie Daley Park**, dedicated in 1983 to a long-time resident and a former principal of Rochester City School No. 13, which is located next to the park. Built in 1903, the brick and stone Horace Mann School was designed by Rochester architect J. Foster Warner. In the 1980s, the building was converted to condominiums.

The intersection of Gregory Street and South Avenue is a city-designated preservation district. A pleasant, post-Civil War commercial streetscape, it is enhanced by a mini-park on the far corner that contributes to the neighborhood's village character.

Turn left onto South Avenue and left at the light onto Averill Avenue. At the corner of Ashland Street, on the left, is the distinctive, brick, Gothic Revival **Calvary St. Andrews Church**, which was completed in 1880 from designs by Richard M. Upjohn of New York City. In the late 1880s, the church was reported to have been the third largest Episcopal parish in western New York, with its congregation comprised largely of workers from the Ellwanger and Barry nursery. Return to Mt. Hope Avenue and turn left.

548-564 Mt. Hope Avenue

Padelt

From Roses to Redwoods

The **Ford St. Bridge** (originally called the Clarissa St. Bridge) lies to the right just past the intersection of Gregory Street and South Avenue. The bridge, built in 1919, marks the start of the Mt. Hope-Highland Preservation District. The restoration of the bridge, including the reconstruction of its entrance pylons, is expected to be completed in 2002.

The heart of Rochester's early reputation as the Flower City starts here, on Mt. Hope Avenue, where German-born George Ellwanger and his Irish partner, Patrick Barry, launched their internationally renowned nursery in 1840 with eight acres of property. Much of the property in what is now the Mt. Hope-Highland Preservation District was owned and developed by these nurserymen.

Ellwanger and Barry's success story was built on hard work and humble origins. Yet the Mt. Hope Nursery almost was destroyed early on by a combination of bad luck and Rochester's weather, which created a test of nearly biblical proportions for the nurserymen. Nature struck hard on the last Sunday in August 1841, when

a hailstorm hit the area, killing many of Ellwanger and Barry's young plants. As if a hailstorm were not enough of a test for the new business, the next day fire broke out in the nursery greenhouse.

Ellwanger and Barry sold the remaining plants to finance the nursery's restoration, and ultimately succeeded in making their business an international success. By 1859, an observer called the Mt. Hope Nurseries "the greatest nursery in the world," praising its cultivation of items such as 120,000 dwarf and standard cherry trees and 5,000 great Sequoias, also known as California Redwood trees. Eventually the nursery included 650 acres of property that stretched from Mt. Hope Avenue to Goodman Street.

Our first contact with buildings from the Ellwanger and Barry era is the group of Gothic Revival "cottages," located on the left at **548**, **554**, **560** and **566 Mt. Hope Avenue** between Linden and Cypress streets. These homes were built in the late 1860s and early 1870s as Ellwanger and Barry branched out into real estate development. They were never workers' houses; the first buyers were professionals. The design of the houses was inspired by the Gothic Revival ideal of architectural author A. J. Downing. Details include steeply pitched cross gables with barge boards, overhanging eaves with bracketed supports, polychrome slate roofs, and distinctive porch trim.

Across the street, at **609 Mt. Hope Avenue**, is the Henry Ellwanger house, built in the early 1870s by the second of George Ellwanger's four sons. Henry helped run the nursery and was the author of *The Rose*, an 1882 treatise that became the standard authority on the subject. He suffered an early death at age 32. Although the house remained in the family until 1982, it was never occupied by Ellwangers after 1906. After being rented, the house was left vacant for 44 years before its renovation by new owners in the early 1980s. The Eastlake-style design is attributed to Rochester architect James G. Cutler. The red brick house features cut-stone sills, a wraparound porch, a slate roof and decorative cutwork barge boards on the steeply-pitched gables.

Next door, at **625 Mt. Hope Avenue**, is the George Ellwanger house, which the co-founder of the Mt. Hope Nurseries purchased in 1867. Designed and built by James Hawks in 1839, this eclectic residence was enlarged by architect Andrew J. Warner for Ellwanger. His son, J. Foster Warner, enlarged the house again in the early 20th century. (For more on the Warners, see Chapter 2.) The house was occupied by members of the Ellwanger family until 1982, when George Ellwanger's granddaughter, Helen Ellwanger, died. Upon her death, Miss Ellwanger, who along with others founded the Landmark Society of Western New York in 1937, left her family estate, including houses at 625 and 609 Mt. Hope Avenue, to the Society. These houses were sold and renovated, but the Society retained ownership of the **Ellwanger Garden**, which had been maintained continuously for 115 years by the Ellwanger family. Not visible from the street, the half-acre garden is located behind the stone wall adjacent to 625 Mt. Hope Avenue. The garden features 25 beds of perennials, which contain memorable collections of peonies, irises and daylilies, plus many less familiar flowering plants. It is open to the public during the Lilac Festival in May, Peony Weekend in June, and by appointment.

The handsome brick residence on the left at **630 Mt. Hope Avenue** was built in 1906 for William C. Barry, Jr., a grandson of nurseryman Patrick Barry and president of the Ellwanger and Barry Realty Company. Designed by J. Foster

Warner, this Georgian Revival house, reflects the success enjoyed by Ellwanger and Barry's descendants as they developed the lush nursery property acquired by the family.

Upon its completion in 1854, the Gothic Revival building at **668 Mt. Hope Avenue** became the office of Mt. Hope Nurseries. Designed by Alexander Jackson Davis, one of America's most influential architects at the time, the building is constructed of brick with a stucco finish that originally was scored to suggest stone. The battlements, which top the square tower, and the triple chimney are among the building's unusual features.

At one time, the grounds around the office were planted with thousands of specimen trees and a grass promenade with 10-foot wide flower borders. Sixteen attached greenhouses served the nursery, along with horse barns, carpenter shops and other buildings.

The rose brick Italianate villa at **692 Mt. Hope Avenue** is the avenue's centerpiece. Built for Patrick Barry, the house was constructed between 1855 and 1857 from plans by the English architect Gervase Wheeler. The residence features a graceful octagonal tower, stone facings and unusual

Patrick Barry House, 692 Mt. Hope Avenue   *Padelt*

eave detail. Nursery co-founder Patrick Barry occupied the house until his death in 1890, and his daughter Harriet Barry Leisching lived there until 1952. The University of Rochester now owns the house, former office, and grounds, which feature more than 90 specimen trees from Ellwanger and Barry's nurseries.

Kettles and Controversy

Shortly ahead, on the right, is **Mt. Hope Cemetery**, a 196-acre arboretum, and the first of America's great Victorian cemeteries developed by a municipality. The cemetery was created in 1832, after a cholera epidemic killed 120 people. Their bodies filled all the available space at downtown burying grounds, leading city officials to seek new space in a less developed area.

The cemetery, with its high ridges and huge depressions called kettles, is one of the area's many remnants of the Ice Age, when the land was covered with a thick layer of ice. Early plans for a cemetery on this unusual property met criticism from Rochesterians such as General Jacob Gould. "Why that ground isn't fit for pasturing rabbits," said Gould, who nonetheless was eventually buried there in a large hillside vault.

Mt. Hope Cemetery Gatehouse   *Padelt*

The present-day Mt. Hope Avenue was named after the cemetery, which was dedicated in 1838. Originally, the avenue was called River Street or South St. Paul.

You can drive through the cemetery on paved roads or park and walk the sloping, landscaped grounds. Designed as parkland to be enjoyed by the living, the cemetery is the resting place of luminaries, including women's rights activist Susan B. Anthony, abolitionist editor and diplomat Frederick Douglass, and George B. Selden, inventor of the automobile engine. Other prominent Rochesterians buried here are city founder Colonel Nathaniel Rochester, and Hiram Sibley, first president of Western Union.

Many of the older gravesites are marked with elaborate funerary sculpture and wrought iron. The Friends of Mt. Hope Cemetery offer guided walking tours on Sunday afternoons, from May through October.

The elaborate north entrance is dominated by the High Victorian Gothic cemetery gatehouse and bell tower at **791 Mt. Hope Avenue**, built in 1874 and designed by Rochester architect Andrew J. Warner. The entrance area was enhanced by the white Moorish Revival gazebo, built in 1872, and the cast-iron Florentine fountain, installed in 1875. Behind the fountain is the original chapel, designed by Henry Searle and erected in 1862. In 1912, the small crematory addition was designed and built by J. Foster Warner.

Drive south beyond the north entrance. Situated on a hill on the left, **Warner Castle** majestically presides over the area. The "castle" was designed and built in 1854 by lawyer, bank president, and newspaper publisher, Horatio Gates Warner, to resemble a Scottish castle of his mother's clan Douglas. For a closer look, turn left onto Reservoir Avenue and left onto Castle Park. The gray stone, castellated structure, as well as the entrance gate and rear gardens, contribute to the picturesque quality of this historic district. Warner Castle is currently owned by the city of Rochester and is leased to the **Rochester Civic Garden Center**. If you park your car here, you can walk behind Warner Castle to a sunken garden. This unusual walled garden, completed around 1930, was designed by Alling DeForest (1875-1957), a noted Rochester landscape architect, who also was responsible for the original landscape at the George Eastman House, as well as the estate of Harvey Firestone, in Akron, Ohio. Restored in 1991 and maintained by the Monroe County Parks Department, DeForest's romantic stone landscape can be admired in all seasons.

A Jagged Silhouette

Castle Park is a picturesque city street that seems like a private driveway. Also on Castle Park you'll find two houses designed by Rochester architect Claude Bragdon. (See Claude Bragdon sidebar, Chapter 2). **"Cro Nest"** at **3 Castle Park**, and closest to Warner Castle, holds a special place among the more than 90 residences designed by one of Rochester's most famous local architects. This was the house the architect designed for himself and his bride, Charlotte Wilkinson, in 1902. Bragdon lived here for 20 years, and his description of its location at the edge of Highland Park remains accurate today. "The house," he wrote, "stands on the brow of a wooded hill overlooking a large city, which appears in winter as a jagged purple silhouette against the northern sky; in summer, nothing of it can be seen, on account of the encompassing trees, the clamorous home of crows and squirrels." The house is distinctive

Warner Castle   *Padelt*

Claude Bragdon

New York Central Railroad Station, 1913 (now demolished)

Claude Bragdon (1866-1946) was Rochester's most innovative early-20th-century architect. He also was an author, a lecturer on art, mysticism, and mathematics, a stage and lighting designer, and a designer of posters, furniture, tile work, and stained glass. In his autobiography, *More Lives Than One*, Bragdon wrote "My life has been driven by a single urge: the desire to discover, to create, or to communicate beauty."

While his professional career spanned 50 years, from 1890 to 1940, his architecture practice in Rochester ended in 1923, when he moved to New York City to pursue his other interests. His own house at 3 Castle Park is an example of his emphasis on natural light, spacious rooms, and craftsman-like details. Bragdon's most notable public building in Rochester is the First Universalist Church, 150 South Clinton Avenue, designed in 1907 in the Lombard Romanesque style, and featuring ornamental terra cotta, stencil patterns, stained glass, and furniture of his creation. His "masterpiece" was the now-demolished 1913 New York Central Railroad Station, an Arts and Crafts building in which he combined a feeling for craftsmanship with a functional expression of the machine age.

for its shingled exterior and complex roof line. Numerous odd-sized and -shaped windows for the attic, stairwell and closet emphasize Bragdon's obsession with natural light.

Bragdon also designed **1 Castle Park** in 1908 for Judge Delbert Hebbard in the Dutch Colonial Revival style, which is characterized by a steeply pitched gambrel roof and dormer windows.

At the end of Castle Park, turn right on Mt. Hope and right on Robinson Drive to take a short tour of Highland Park.

Highland Park

Highland Park is Ellwanger and Barry's most spectacular legacy. The park contains an internationally renowned collection of lilacs and lesser-known gems such as the pinetum (pi-NEE-tum), an arboretum of evergreen trees offering, in the middle of the city, dense shade with the tart scent of pine.

Rochester's first park, designed by world-famous landscape architect Frederick Law Olmsted, was established in 1888 with 20 acres of land donated to the city by the nursery owners.

Frederick Douglass

World famous Highland Park, with its unsurpassed collection of lilacs, also is home to the relocated Frederick Douglass monument. Douglass, one of Rochester's most famous residents, spent 25 of his most productive years in Rochester. The monument, dedicated in 1898 after Douglass's death, originally was located at St. Paul Street and Central Avenue.

Frederick Douglass's contribution to the abolitionist movement and the civil rights of African-Americans is unsurpassed. Born in 1818 (earlier sources say 1817) in Maryland, Douglass escaped slavery in 1838 and soon gained renown as an anti-slavery lecturer and writer. After lecturing as an agent of the American Anti-slavery Society, Douglass arrived in Rochester in 1847 and began publishing his anti-slavery newspaper, *The North Star*, opening a downtown office in the Talman Block, 25 East Main Street (see Chapter 2).

While in Rochester, Douglass also became active in the women's rights movement and was a friend of Susan B. Anthony. Douglass; his two wives; Anna Murray Douglass and Helen Pitts Douglass; and his daughter, Annie, are buried in Mt. Hope Cemetery.

Lamberton Conservatory   *Olenick*

The park expanded with the acquisition of additional acres along the western portion of the Pinnacle Hills and with property donated by the Warner estate. It now encompasses 155 acres.

Highland Park's design represents a compromise between the arboretum desired by its nurserymen donors and the glacial pastoral landscape preferred by Olmsted (see sidebar, Chapter 2). This park includes winding paths that take advantage of the hills and lofty views. South-facing slopes became an arboretum, or "tree garden," for trees and shrubs, some of which were donated from Ellwanger and Barry's nurseries.

Near the end of Robinson Drive, on the right, is the **Highland Bowl**, used in summer for theater and musical performances. Statues of abolitionist Frederick Douglass (see sidebar, this chapter) and the German poet and dramatist Johann Wolfgang von Goethe (1749-1832) overlook the bowl.

Take a right on South Avenue and a left on Reservoir Drive. On the left is **Lamberton Conservatory**, named after park commissioner and later president of the Parks board, Alexander

Lamberton. The conservatory was opened to great fanfare in 1911. Renovated and expanded, the conservatory is open to the public and features varied climatic exhibits and ever-changing seasonal floral displays. The greenhouses surround a goldfish pond and planting area.

Continue on Reservoir Drive past the reservoir to the right. Just past the Gate House, on the crest of the hill, once stood a round, wooden, three-story pavilion erected in 1890 to raise people above the treeline and provide a 360-degree vista of the surrounding country. It was a gift of George Ellwanger and Patrick Barry to the children of Rochester, and was dedicated to all Rochester children who had died of cholera or other diseases. By 1967, it was deemed unsafe and was demolished.

Bear right onto Pinetum Drive. The pinetum contains a collection of about 300 species of cone-bearing trees and shrubs, including pines, spruces, hemlocks and firs.

At the intersection of South Goodman Street, look across the street to the wooded hillside site of **Colgate-Rochester-Drexel Divinity School**.

The dramatic English Gothic tower, which may be visible through the trees, is part of a consolidated group of campus buildings designed by James Gambel Rogers, a prominent collegiate architect, and constructed in 1930-31 with funds donated by John D. Rockefeller.

Turn right on South Goodman and right again onto Highland Avenue. To the right is the famous lilac collection, which was started in 1892 by John Dunbar, Rochester's first superintendent of parks. The collection comprises about 1,200 shrubs stretching across 22 acres. Many of the more than 500 varieties were introduced and created in Rochester. The lilacs have been the focus of an annual Lilac Festival since 1905.

Continue on Highland Avenue, crossing South Avenue, to Mt. Hope Avenue and turn left. Mt. Hope Cemetery continues on the right, and soon you will pass the south cemetery entrance, which is dominated by the late-Gothic Revival chapel, designed by J. Foster Warner and completed in 1912.

A right turn on Elmwood Avenue takes you past the University of Rochester School of Medicine and Dentistry on the left. The distinctive, angular, brick **Eastman Dental Center**, at **625 Elmwood Avenue**, was built in 1978 and designed by Richard Foster of Greenwich, Connecticut. Foster is known for his works at Yale and New York universities, as well as at Lincoln Center.

The pastiche of modern and older buildings seen from Elmwood Avenue is a far cry from the original two-story research building constructed in August 1922. At that time, Elmwood Avenue was unpaved and neglected by city snow-removal crews. The isolation of the place was vividly described by Dr. George Whipple, a Nobel Prize winner and first director of the School of Medicine. He wrote: "The drive from Mt. Hope Avenue was always an adventure reminding one of pioneering above the Arctic Circle.... Snow plows were reported but never seen."

The original medical school-hospital complex, one of the first to combine all facilities under one roof, opened in 1925 and covered one-and-a-half acres. It also was a reflection of benefactor George Eastman's aesthetic sense. Eastman required that the new school be devoid of elaborate detail.

Eastman Dental Center   *Petronio*

To emphasize that point, he drove Edwin Gordon, one of the architects for the new school, past Kodak Park and said: "That's what we want. No fancy stuff." The utilitarian building is a massive, red brick edifice with little ornamental detail. While Eastman was satisfied, university trustee and architect James G. Cutler called its style "Early Penitentiary Period."

On the right is the edge of the **University of Rochester River Campus**, which, today, includes about 6,000 graduate and undergraduate students. The population is a far cry from the 82 students who entered in 1850, the university's first year. At that time, the fledgling institution of higher learning was housed in the former United States Hotel in downtown Rochester, (see Chapter 4). Tuition was $10 a term, or $30 a year, and professors received an annual salary of $1,200.

The university moved the men's college to the River Campus in 1930 after outgrowing its original Prince Street campus (see Chapter 1). The women's college remained on Prince Street until the men's and women's colleges merged on the River Campus in 1955. Oak Hill Country Club had owned the pastoral, riverside land on which the River Campus was built. The country club ultimately moved to a Pittsford site after a successful community fundraising campaign enabled the university to purchase the 82 acres of riverfront property. While university officials praised the potential for a spacious new campus, some city officials grumbled at the prospect. "Educate 'em the old way," grumbled former Rochester Mayor Hiram H. Edgerton. "They need no swimming hole. A bath on Saturday night is enough...."

For a brief detour of the University's River Campus, turn right onto Wilson Boulevard, just beyond the railroad underpass. Continue straight, past the information booth. Designed by Gordon and Kaelber, with the assistance of Frederick Law Olmsted, Jr., Charles Adams Platt and others, the formal quadrangle (on the right) and original campus buildings are Colonial Revival, with a few Renaissance touches, exemplified by the handsome dome of **Rush Rhees Library**, located at the end of the quadrangle. Among the more modern buildings added to the campus is the 1976 **Wilson Commons**, designed by internationally renowned architect I. M. Pei. This glass-fronted building is visible on the right from the loop, which will take you back to Elmwood Avenue.

Return to Elmwood Avenue, and at the light, continue straight onto Moore Drive, the entrance to Genesee Valley Park. The view of the Genesee River to the right is one of many enduring aspects of the park.

Genesee Valley Park

Frederick Law Olmsted created the park as an English-style pastoral landscape, which he defined as large, open meadows with groups of trees or scattered individual trees. More than 91,480 trees and shrubs were planted in the park between 1889 and 1901. Throughout the park were winding pleasure drives and riverside pathways, giving the visitor ever-changing views of the river and meadows. The meadows of Genesee Valley Park were so extensive that sheep were allowed to graze in order to trim the lawns.

Near the park entrance, on the left, is a statue of Dr. Edward Mott Moore (1814-1902), a surgeon at St. Mary's Hospital and president of the American Medical Association in 1890. Moore is best known as the founder of Rochester's parks system and was president of the Parks Commission. Farther along, on the left, is a large, two-story dovecote – a pigeon roost – similar to one located in Maplewood Rose Garden (see Chapter 2).

Continue over the canal and expressway, then turn left. The s-curving road employs a typical Olmsted device intended to showcase a changing landscape. By designing a road where the end point is not visible, Olmsted enhanced the mystery of the route. For a closer look at the park, turn right at the stop sign and park.

Originally the park was designed so that the western side of the river would be used for active recreation. Over time, recreational activities were incorporated into the east side of the park. These include a polo grounds, now used for track meets, tennis courts, and two 18-hole golf courses. Other areas have been developed as picnic areas that can hold thousands of people.

Since its creation, the park has undergone considerable changes. Between 1912 and 1914, the Erie Canal was rerouted through the middle of the park, severing the circulation of the park as designed in 1890. The Olmsted Brothers were hired by the New York State Canal Board to reconnect the park circulation and to provide pedestrian bridges, which still gracefully cross the canal. The elevation of formerly prominent Red Creek, a tributary of the Genesee River, was changed to accommodate the water level of the canal. Subsequently, the Red Creek Valley, located north of the canal and originally a scenic waterway dotted with small islands, was lost.

Genesee Valley Park was compromised more seriously in 1979 by the construction of Interstate 390. The expressway was constructed through its heart, sweeping away trees and picnic areas, and adding the steady hum of high-speed traffic, thereby destroying much of the serenity of the pastoral landscape. To accommodate the various changes, the main circulation road designed by Olmsted also was altered. Two public golf courses, the old course and the new, now occupy the meadow designed by Frederick Law Olmsted. However, the park retains a good deal of charm and continues to offer an oasis of open green space with mature trees within the city.

The road over Red Creek is now closed to vehicular traffic, but you can view it after you exit the park. Return to the stop sign and proceed right to East River Road. Turn right onto East River Road and continue slowly, looking right as you cross over Red Creek to catch a glimpse of one of Genesee Valley Park's original bridges.

Genesee Valley Park   *Olenick*

East River Road is one of our area's earliest north-south routes. First used by Native Americans, it was later opened to connect early Rochesterville with older settlements to the south. Late-19th- and early-20th-century houses in the area are survivors of massive floods that damaged the neighborhood in 1927 and 1936, prior to construction of the Mt. Morris Dam. Along here, you'll also pass the Genesee Valley Park's golf courses and its 1929 clubhouse on the right.

After entering the town of Brighton, you'll soon come to a historic standout among houses in the area – the Greek Revival farmhouse at **1564 East River Road**. The wood clapboard-sided structure was constructed about 1842, during a period (1830-1850) when Greek Revival domestic architecture flourished. Notable features include the frieze windows with original iron grilles, a wide cornice with gable-end returns, cobblestone foundation, and the front entrance surround with flanking pilasters supporting a wide entablature.

Continue on, past the highly visible, original **West Shore Railroad Bridge** (later New York Central, now Conrail). Spanning 232 feet across the Genesee River, this steel bridge with triangular trusses was built in 1905 by the Riter Conley Manufacturing Company of Pittsburgh.

Take a left at the intersection of East River and Jefferson roads to see the **Rochester Institute of Technology** (RIT) campus, a showcase of mid-20th-century architecture constructed in 1968. The main entrance to the campus is the first right turn off Jefferson Road. Due to the layout of the sprawling institution, many of the buildings are impossible to see by car.

You can get a cursory glance by taking the circular drive around the campus, or you can experience it on foot after attempting to park in a campus lot.

RIT traces its history to 1829, when the Rochester Athenaeum was created as a group sponsoring lectures, book reviews and cultural discussions. A more direct predecessor was the Mechanics Institute, founded in 1885 by a group of Rochester industrialists as a school of technical training. The institute, which consolidated with the Rochester Athenaeum in 1891, has since offered a combination of technology and arts courses. Its earliest courses, offered on South Fitzhugh Street in Rochester, ranged from mechanical and freehand drawing to china painting and clay modeling. The Institute was renamed Rochester Institute of Technology in 1944, and began granting degrees in 1953.

The unconventional and controversial RIT campus opened on its 1,300-acre property following a collaborative effort by some of the era's most prominent architects, including principal coordinating architect Lawrence B. Anderson; Edward Larrabee Barnes; Kevin Roche and John Dinkeloo; Hugh Stubbins and Harry M. Weese. Landscape architect Dan Kiley also helped design the campus.

The brick architecture, a unifying element of the campus, is powerful and untraditional, with nary a pediment or classical column in sight. The buildings were conceived as "weighty sculptural objects, intentionally monumental and heroic," RIT professor Houghton Wetherald has observed. The architecture of the campus won the American Institute of Architects' Collaboration in Architecture Award for 1972. Yet the style, called Brutalism, also has been criticized widely. The campus initially was nicknamed "Bricksville," wrote Anderson. Wetherald has written that there is "a kind of paramilitary flavor which characterizes the campus ... its sense of mass order and individual disorientation."

After viewing the campus, return to the main entrance and take a left turn back onto Jefferson Road. Cross over the river and turn left onto Scottsville Road (Rt. 383).

Scottsville Road marks the beginning of a long-time farming area. About three miles down the road, carefully tended fences on the right mark the first of several horse farms in the area. Just past Brook Road, the road winds up a hill, which was once called Dumpling Hill, named in honor of the delicious dumplings prepared and sold to fishermen by a woman who once lived here. It also has been called Doubling Hill, because it was so difficult to ascend that early settlers hauling grain to Rochester mills needed to double up their teams of horses to climb the hill.

Just beyond the hill, on the left, at **2262 Scottsville Road**, is a fine Queen Anne residence, built c. 1888, that was the home of Louis A. Wehle. He reorganized Genesee Brewing Company (now High Falls Brewing Company) in 1933, after the company had stopped manufacturing during prohibition. The brewery was established in 1878 on the east bank of the Genesee River, across from Brown's Race (see Chapter 2). Wehle was a horseman who bred, raised, and raced trotting horses. He built an elegant brick stable, located just beyond the house on the right, where he kept his twelve-horse draft team, which pulled the brewery wagon. Notice the draft-horse weather-vane on the cupola.

Farther along, you'll soon come to the small **Chili Cobblestone School**, on the right, at **2517 Scottsville Road**, an artifact from another era. Just beyond the building there is a small parking lot where you may wish to stop. Erected in 1848, the building served as a one-room schoolhouse until 1952. In the early days, one teacher taught eight grades and served as her own custodian. Today, the town of Chili owns and maintains the restored schoolhouse as a museum, which is open to the public. The cobblestone schoolhouse is an example of one of western New York's most distinctive 19th-century construction types. (See sidebar on cobblestone architecture, Chapter 5)

Rich Harvest

Just beyond the New York State Thruway over-pass, you enter the town of Wheatland. During the early and middle 1800s, Wheatland had a reputation for growing some of the highest-quality wheat in the country. One explanation for the fine wheat suggests that the frequent flooding of the Genesee River and Oatka Creek provided abundant fertilization from fish and other organic matter. Wheat was shipped to the Erie Canal by the Genesee Valley Canal, and later, by the Scottsville-Caledonia Railroad.

Wheatland's 19th-century prosperity is reflected in the village of Scottsville's well-maintained historic buildings. The village was named after Isaac Scott from New Hampshire, who purchased 150 acres of land for $4 per acre and built a log house in 1790.

Scott was not the first settler, however. In 1786, Ebenezer Allan built a log cabin on a knoll on the northern bank of Oatka Creek, near the creek's intersection with the Genesee River. Allan, a kind of Daniel Boone of the Genesee Valley, traded with the Indians and married a Seneca woman, earning him the nickname "Indian." In 1790, Allan sold his farm, moved north, and built first a sawmill, and later a gristmill, on the west bank of the Genesee near the falls in present-day downtown Rochester. By 1794, however, Allan had left, and the mills were abandoned.

Greek Revival Village

Route 383 leads into Rochester Street, a National Register and village-designated historic district. Over half of the buildings date from the period of the 1830s to the 1850s, stamping the village street with an overall "Greek Revival" character. Scottsville resident, Carl Schmidt (1894-1988), an architect, and author and illustrator of more than 18 books on local architecture, once described these dwellings as "the homes of doctors, ministers, merchants and craftsmen. They are not mansions, but modest dwellings in the varied styles of the nineteenth century with good proportion, interesting details, fine mouldings and excellent craftsmanship."

The prominent Greek Revival house on the right, at **7 Rochester Street**, was originally owned by Dr. Freeman Edson, a nephew of village founder Isaac Scott. First erected in 1816, additions and updates in 1846 are responsible for the Greek Revival details of the house, including corner pilasters and gracious wood grills in a frieze band.

Across the street, at **No. 10**, was Schmidt's home, the handsome Greek Revival residence

7 Rochester Street   *Padelt*

built in 1830, with the tall windows and the decorative cast-iron fence, both features of an 1850 update.

Bear right onto **Main Street**. The best way to see the village is to park on the street or in the municipal lot, off to the right, and walk. Across the street, at **No. 1**, is a long, two-story frame commercial structure, with a decorative porch that dates from 1881, and sits on the original site of Isaac Scott's tavern. In the 1890s, this building served as an ice cream parlor and catered to bicyclists traveling the Rochester- to-Scottsville bike path, a route inaugurated by 1500 bicycle riders on September 12, 1896. On the right, at **Nos. 8-16**, is a row of modest structures, mostly Greek Revival in style, that represents a rare survivor of an early 19th-century commercial streetscape. The cobblestone building at **No. 14** was built as a general store in 1838, and features cast-iron storefront pilasters added in the 1890s.

Just past the modern fire hall, on the right, at **28 Main Street**, is the picturesque **Scottsville Free Library** designed with Queen Anne elements by Scottsville architect Charles Ellis. Built in 1892 as Windom Hall, the building originally served as a public meeting space,

theater, and dance hall. The Scottsville Free Library, established in 1805 and the first library west of the Genesee River, moved here in 1916. Listed in the National Register of Historic Places, the building features an intact Victorian interior with oiled tongue-and-groove wood walls and ceiling; it is well worth a visit. The stage, restored in 2000 as a reading area, is a war memorial to Scottsville citizens who gave their lives from the Revolutionary War to World War II.

Another Charles Ellis building can be found next door at **30 Main Street**. Once known as the General Merchandise Store, this tall, narrow building incorporates Queen Anne details, including fish scale shingles on the second story, and an oriel window projecting over the first-floor storefront.

Now take a right onto one-way **Church Street** and enjoy an attractive grouping of modest, brick-and-frame, Greek Revival dwellings that were built between 1828 and 1840. At the stop sign, look left at the fine Greek Revival entrance at **No. 17**, with its beautiful door carved with Greek motifs.

In the next block, the street becomes **Browns Avenue** and passes two distinguished churches. The stately frame **Union Presbyterian Church** on the left, at **No. 1**, was built in 1857 in the similar style of an earlier church, which was erected in 1822 and destroyed by fire. The brick "**Masonic Temple**," next door, was built as a schoolhouse in 1869.

The third building on the left is the 1885 **Grace Episcopal Church**, one of Scottsville's architectural gems. The church is the work of prominent local architects Harvey and Charles Ellis, who were asked to follow the designs popularized by the noted Boston architect, H. H. Richardson. The church is cruciform in plan, with the lower sections sculpted of rough cobbles and fieldstone. Above this rises a contrasting curtain wall of red wood shingles and colorful stained glass windows of delicately sketched abstract and geometric designs. Notice the dramatic sloping hood on the front porch and the low-reaching roof overall, which is sometimes sharply angled, sometimes softly curved.

Turn around and drive back to Main Street by taking a right on Race Street, which leads directly to Main Street. The brick houses in this area

Grace Episcopal Church   *Padelt*

around Main Street were built in the early 19th-century from bricks manufactured in the village. Turn right onto **Main Street**. A short distance on the left, at **No. 69**, is the diminutive, one-story 1830 **Sage-Marlowe House and Skivington Research Library**. This simple, frame Greek Revival former residence, renovated by the Wheatland Historical Association, contains local historical documents and is open by appointment.

Leaving Scottsville, take Route 383 South (Scottsville-Mumford Road) to continue the tour to Mumford and Genesee Country Museum. About two miles from Scottsville, at the intersection of Union Street, is the hamlet of **Garbutt**, named after the family who settled here. The once-prosperous four corners had stores and a school, as well as the Garbutt family homes, of which several remain nearby. One of the most charming structures here is the tiny Greek Revival building on the left at **1013 Scottsville-Mumford Road**, which was built as a tailor shop.

Garbutt also was the center of an active gypsum industry, which eventually closed in the mid-20th century. During the second half of the 19th century, Oatka Creek, which parallels Scottsville-Mumford Road, was lined with mills. At one time, there were six mills grinding wheat, four mills grinding gypsum for making plaster of Paris, and two mills sawing logs.

Also parallel to the road are the tracks of the present Rochester & Southern Railroad, which was used to transport gypsum.

Shortly after the intersection of Belcoda Road, where the Oatka Creek flows close to the road on the left, there is a log cabin, at **2389 Scottsville-Mumford Road**, which was built in 1803 by a Scotsman, Findley McArthur, and renovated in the early 1900s.

Route 383 takes a sweeping turn south into the hamlet of Mumford. Like Scottsville and Garbutt, Mumford prospered during the 19th century from grist, woolen, plaster, and paper mills, as well as breweries and distilleries, which were powered by Oatka Creek. At the flashing light, on the northwest corner of **Main** and **George streets**, stands the 1835 brick former **Exchange Hotel**. One of several 19th-century inns in the county, it has been restored and adapted to house a store and the local fire department. Notice the door on the George Street side, which traditionally led into a tavern room.

Turn right onto George Street. On the left is the handsome Gothic Revival **First Presbyterian Church of Mumford**, built from 1870 to 1883. Constructed of a rare "bog" limestone quarried from a nearby farm, the church was described in Ripley's *Believe It or Not* as the church "built entirely of wood that turned to stone."

On the right, at **948 George Street**, is a cut-stone residence that originally served as one of early Mumford's mill operations. Built in 1833 by Philip Garbutt as a plaster mill, it later was used in the manufacture of hubs, handles, and wheel spokes. In the early 1900s, the Gardner Paper Company purchased the structure and converted it to a residence for the company's plant manager.

George Street becomes Flint Hill Road and leads to the **Genesee Country Village and Museum**, a re-creation of 19th-century life in Upstate New York with 57 restored and furnished buildings and open to the public. Buildings moved to the museum include the 1797 Amherst-Humphrey House from Lima; the 1844 Greek Revival Brooks Grove Methodist Church and Parsonage; and the 1847 birthplace of George Eastman from Waterville. The late 1800s buildings at the museum, such as the 1870 octagon house from Friendship, New York, are larger and more elaborate than the earlier houses on the property.

City life is interpreted in the elegant Livingston-Backus House, built in 1827 and originally located in the Third Ward (now Corn Hill) in Rochester. The house was built by James K. Livingston, an attorney and land speculator, four years after the Erie Canal opened in Rochester, creating a demand for real estate. Recently restored after a 1996 fire, the elegant interior is a testimony to prosperous 19th-century Rochester, America's boomtown flush with the Erie Canal's success.

Also worth a visit are the museum's John L. Wehle's Gallery of Sporting Art and the Nature Center, as well as a variety of special events held throughout the year.

Westward to Brockport
Following the Canal

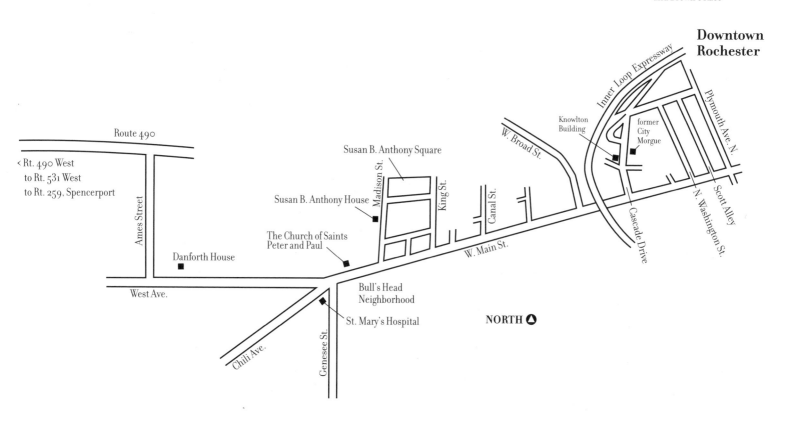

Frontier Field
and Brown's Race

**Downtown
Rochester**

Inner Loop Expressway

Route 490

< Rt. 490 West
to Rt. 531 West
to Rt. 259, Spencerport

W. Broad St.

Knowlton
Building

former
City
Morgue

Plymouth Ave. N.

Susan B. Anthony Square

Madison St.

Scott Alley

N. Washington St.

Susan B. Anthony House

King St.

Canal St.

Ames Street

Cascade Drive

Danforth House

The Church of Saints
Peter and Paul

W. Main St.

West Ave.

Bull's Head
Neighborhood

NORTH

Chili Ave.

Genesee St.

St. Mary's Hospital

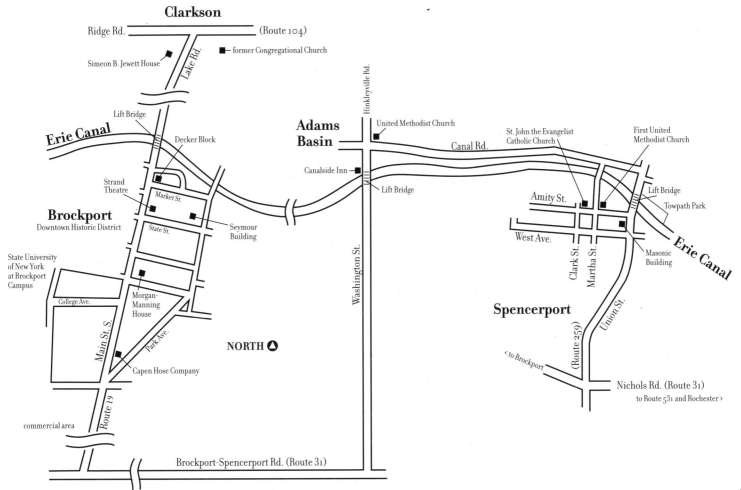

Clarkson

Ridge Rd. (Route 104)

■ former Congregational Church

Simeon B. Jewett House

Lake Rd.

Lift Bridge

Decker Block

Erie Canal

Strand
Theatre

Market St.

Brockport
Downtown Historic District

State St.

Seymour
Building

State University
of New York
at Brockport
Campus

College Ave.

Morgan-
Manning
House

Park Ave.

Main St. S.

NORTH ⬣

Capen Hose Company

Route 19

commercial area

Brockport-Spencerport Rd. (Route 31)

Hinkleyville Rd.

**Adams
Basin**

United Methodist Church
■

Canalside Inn ■

Lift Bridge

Canal Rd.

Washington St.

St. John the Evangelist
Catholic Church

First United
Methodist Church

Amity St.
■
■

Lift Bridge

Towpath Park

West Ave.

Clark St.

Martha St.

Masonic
Building

Erie Canal

Spencerport

Union St.

< to Brockport

(Route 259)

Nichols Rd. (Route 31)

to Route 531 and Rochester >

This tour begins in Rochester's Cascade Historic District, proceeds west through Spencerport and Brockport, and ends in Clarkson.

Mileage: Approximately 40 miles, including optional detour to Springdale Farm

Time: Approximately two hours

~ Open to the Public ~

Susan B. Anthony House
19 Madison Street, Rochester, phone 235-6124

Western Monroe Historical Society
151 South Main Street, Brockport, phone 637-3645

Emily Knapp Local History Museum & Library,
49 State Street, Brockport, phone 637-5300

Springdale Farm
696 Colby Street, Spencerport, phone 352-5315

Ogden Historical Society Museum
568 Colby Street, Spencerport, phone 352-1586

The sisters were dressed for autumn.

With bonnets covering their hair, Hannah Mosher, and Mary and Susan B. Anthony walked deliberately from their homes at 17 and 19 Madison Street, to a polling place at the corner of West Avenue (now West Main Street) and Prospect Street.

Registering to vote was simple enough for a man of the era. But on November 1, 1872, the Anthony sisters rocked the course of history by signing up to vote. Before the year was out, Susan B. Anthony would vote and encourage others to cast ballots in the general election. She would be handcuffed, set free on bail, and ultimately fined for violating the law. At the trial, she lamented, "this high-handed outrage upon my citizen's rights."

Yet the sisters' walk that November 1 encouraged a fight for women's suffrage that would not be successful until the ratification of the 19th amendment to the Constitution in 1920 – too late for Susan B. Anthony. The efforts of Susan B. Anthony, who lived in Rochester throughout her adult life, also fueled a continuing movement for women's rights.

Starting in the Cascade Historic District (the popular name for the National Register District, Bridge Square) several blocks east of Anthony's home, this tour travels west via West Main Street and West Avenue through a downtown commercial area prominent during much of the 19th century. It continues westward through the Erie Canal villages of Spencerport and Brockport before exploring the landmark-rich hamlet of Clarkson.

Barges, trains and railroad stations

There is a sense of time frozen in the Cascade Historic District, where buildings were built at a frenzied pace until 1918, when the Erie Canal was rerouted, taking it away from downtown Rochester. First established as a residential neighborhood, the district, bounded on the north and west by the Inner Loop Expressway, on the south by West Main Street, and on the east by North Washington Street, became a center for commercial development after the Erie Canal opened in the 1820s. As other parts of the city seized the imagination of builders after 1917, the Cascade Historic District has remained solidly rooted in an earlier era.

The tour begins at a modest building with a rich history of its own, the former United States Hotel on the right at **212-214 West Main Street**. This L-shaped, Federal-style building proudly displays on the facade "1826," the year of its construction. The oldest surviving commercial building in the central business district, the hotel originally was located about 70 yards from the north bank of the Erie Canal, now Broad Street. The hotel was built at a time when Rochester, the "Young Lion of the West," was becoming America's first boomtown. Yet it failed to attract guests. By 1850, it had been converted to a manual training school and a girls' school.

Next, the building would serve as an incubator for two leading educational institutions in modern-day Rochester. In 1850, the fledgling

University of Rochester briefly leased, then purchased the former hotel for its first campus. Students lived on the upper floors, while the lower floors included a library and lecture halls. In 1850, the University rented some of its space there to another new educational institution – the Rochester Theological Seminary, which would later become the current Colgate-Rochester-Crozer Divinity School.

From West Main Street, take a right on Cascade Drive, an urban sanctuary of historic industrial buildings. Immediately on the left, on the corner of West Main and Cascade, is the former **J. Hungerford Smith Building** at **242 West Main Street**. It is one of many buildings on West Main Street of brick construction and in scale with the United States Hotel. This building was constructed in 1895 for the manufacture of syrups, extracts and flavorings. Characteristic of the Chicago-style of commercial architecture, the four-story masonry structure features a corbeled and denticulated brick cornice and large brick pilasters between the bays.

Also on the left, just past the Smith Building, is the five-story **Knowlton Building**, at **No. 69 Cascade Drive**, originally a paper box factory.

Knowlton Building   *Petronio*

Now adapted for commercial and residential uses, this first section of the building was built beginning in 1895, with the second section erected in 1905. Embossed in a decorative panel, the building's name and date can be found in the pediment above the front entrance.

Across the street, to the right, the most ornate of the Cascade Drive buildings was constructed in 1905 to house the dead. The former city morgue, at **Nos. 66-70**, a meticulously detailed brick building, is modified Italian Renaissance-commercial style. The first floor has four round-arched windows and radiating voussoirs. The second story has corbeled round arches over the windows and a series of repeating small brick arches in the frieze. Horse stalls and stables originally were located in the rear of the building, now renovated for commercial use.

On the left, next to the expressway, the **Daily Record Building** at **39-43 Cascade Drive** was constructed as a factory in 1915 and has had a long association with the printing industry. It is highlighted by tripartite double-hung windows, brick pilasters, and an open-air corner patio for a second-story apartment.

Continue to follow Cascade Drive, which curves to the right, then turn immediately right on North Washington Street. Located here is a group of commercial buildings erected in the 1880s. On the right, at **25-27 North Washington Street**, is the Keeler and Nichols Building, a former carriage factory, with its asymmetrical Romanesque-style facade. Across the street, to the left, is a distinctive brick building at **30-32 North Washington Street**. Listed in the National Register of Historic Places, it is one of the city's few surviving examples of early-19th-century rowhouse architecture.

Return to West Main Street. Turn right on West Main, drive west and pass under the Route 490 expressway bridge.

"Like a thing of life"

While the Erie Canal dominated Rochester life in the early 1800s, railroads captured the imagination of the public by the mid-1800s, leading more people and freight to be carried by rail than by water. The former **Buffalo, Rochester and Pittsburgh Railroad Station**, on the right, at **320 West Main Street**, is a monument to the bustling rail center that once was a part of the neighborhood. This massive, red-brick building with roof-top towers was constructed in 1881-1882 as a passenger depot. Notable features are patterned brickwork, terra cotta tiles, and scalloped brickwork designs.

Rochester's railroad history began in this neighborhood on May 11, 1837. On that day, to the cheers of spectators, the Tonawanda Railroad launched the city's first rail service. Luminaries from the community boarded that first train at tracks near the United States Hotel. A local reporter said the train engine was "panting like an impatient war-horse" and sped forward "like a thing of life" on its 32-mile trip to Batavia, encountering cheering crowds along the way. By 1860, there were 60 trains leaving the city each day, and numerous competing train companies.

Continue on West Main Street. On the right, just after Trowbridge Street, was the beginning of the Genesee Valley Canal, a 107-mile waterway that extended from the Erie Canal in Rochester, south along the Genesee River to Olean and the Southern Tier. The Genesee Valley Canal, which opened in 1840, was ultimately abandoned in 1878, a victim of changing times and the popularity of the railroad. Today, Canal Street, on the right, is the sole reminder of this defunct waterway.

You are now entering a neighborhood that is a city-designated preservation district and listed in the National Register of Historic Places. Easy access to the railroad, as well as the Erie and Genesee Valley canals, helped spur commercial development of this area. **The Madison Square-West Main Street Historic District**, known as the Susan B. Anthony neighborhood, includes everything from Susan B. Anthony's home to a large, industrial carriage-manufacturing complex.

To the right, just off West Main Street and beyond the lumber storage yard, is a group of brick buildings along the west side of Canal Street. This is what remains of the once-massive James Cunningham, Son and Co. carriage-manufacturing complex. Though horse-drawn carriages have become as obsolete as ice boxes, at its peak, Cunningham's factory rivaled present-day Eastman Kodak as an influential force in Rochester life. By 1850, the carriage factory built by this Irish immigrant was the largest of its kind in New York state, selling 700 carriages per year at $200 apiece. By the 1880s, it was the city's largest employer, with over 800 workers.

On the right, between Canal and King streets, is a distinctive row of 19th- and early-20th-century commercial buildings that for much of the last 150 years served as the retail hub for this neighborhood. Across the street, the property on the south side of West Main Street, opposite King Street, held a central role in Rochester's history. Now a residential neighborhood, it was the site of West Cemetery, a local burial ground, in the early 19th century. In 1864, patients replaced gravestones as the new Rochester City Hospital was constructed here. Burial remains were moved to the new municipal cemetery at Mt. Hope (see Chapter 3), and the City Hospital became the second in the community after nearby St. Mary's Hospital. Eventually renamed Rochester General Hospital, the institution continued here into the 1960s when it relocated to Portland Avenue and the hospital buildings here were demolished.

Continue one block and turn right on Madison Street. This compact neighborhood is unique in the city. It is the only surviving example of an early-19th-century tract that has retained its original public square and the layout of its streets and alleyways. Its importance in the late 19th century can be gauged by the people who lived

there, including industrialists, a Rochester mayor, and the internationally known suffragist Susan B. Anthony. The best way to experience this neighborhood is to walk around and see the range of architectural styles here, ranging from the 1830s to the 1920s.

On your left, at **17 Madison Street**, is the modest brick house that was the home of Susan B. Anthony from 1866 until her death in 1906. Tours of the house are offered from the **Education and Visitor Center of the Susan B. Anthony House**, next door at **No. 19**, the former home of Susan's sister, Hannah A. Mosher.

Also on the left is one of the many notable residences in the neighborhood, **27 Madison Street**, a brick Italianate built by factory-owner Stephen Coleman, whose family continued to reside here for 100 years. Built in 1857 at a cost of $3,500, this house has a large cupola, louvered shutters, and a large yard with distinctive gardens and landscaping.

Pull over and park your car along the curb next to the park square. Imagine how the residents of this secluded residential enclave have used this landscaped oasis for recreation and relaxation over the past two centuries. First laid out in the

Susan B. Anthony House   *Olenick*

Susan B. Anthony

Susan B. Anthony (1820-1906) devoted her life to the battle for women's rights. Born in Adams, Massachusetts, Anthony became the best-known advocate for the rights of women, touring the country in her single-minded quest to have women and men treated equally.

Anthony moved to Rochester in 1845 with her family, where her father, Daniel, purchased a 32-acre farm and a Greek Revival farmhouse at what is now Genesee Park Boulevard and Brooks Avenue. After Daniel died, Susan's sister Mary and her mother moved to the city and bought the house at 17 Madison Street, which became Susan's home and refuge from her busy schedule and travels for the rest of her life.

Built in 1859, the house, one of only two National Historic Landmarks in Rochester, was visited by such famous contemporaries as Elizabeth Cady Stanton and abolitionist Frederick Douglass (see Chapter 3). In 1897, the roof was raised and the added third floor became Susan's office. It is filled today with personal belongings and memorabilia from her long and productive life.

In her later years, Susan maintained a strenuous schedule of lectures and public appearances. Now a celebrity, she was widely honored, both in Rochester and throughout the United States. Near the end of her life, Anthony encouraged her fellow suffragettes to believe that "Failure is impossible." When she died, flags were flown at half-mast, the first time a woman's death had been so marked in Rochester.

Mary Anthony, 1827-1907, sister of Susan, a prominent Rochester educator and women's rights activist in her own right, working out of her home at 17 Madison Street. While Susan operated on a national sphere, Mary focused most of her attention on women in Rochester. Mary worked as a teacher and a principal in the Rochester City Schools. She insisted on earning a salary equal to the male principals, and became the first woman to achieve this right. Her work as founder of the Women's Political Club of Rochester in 1885 helped persuade local officials to appoint women to positions in the police department and other areas of government. Mary Anthony also broke the law in protest many times, including the time she voted with her sister, and in her decision to withhold taxes for more than a decade as a protest against inequality.

"Let's Have Tea," bronze sculpture by Pepsy M. Kettavong   *Petronio*

1830s as Mechanic Square, it was renamed Madison Park in 1875. This small-scale park is typical of the compact urban park squares that dotted Rochester in the early 19th century. Designed as an open square, the curved sidewalks and silver maple trees were added to the park by the Olmsted Brothers landscaping firm in 1904. The park was renamed **Susan B. Anthony Square** in 1971, and renovated again in the early 1980s. *"Let's Have Tea,"* a bronze sculpture of Susan B. Anthony and Frederick Douglass, by Pepsy M. Kettavong, is a recent addition to the square.

On the left, opposite the park, is the earliest Greek Revival house in the district at **37 Madison Street**. Built in the 1840s, the brick building features stone lintels, wide cornices, an oculus gable window, and a rectangular transom over the front entrance.

On the right, at the corner of Madison Park North, the 1850 brick Italianate residence at **42 Madison Street** has a cupola with round-arched windows, as well as stone lintels, sills and watertable. With its distinctive site overlooking the park, this house included among its early owners a confectioner in the 1880s and a saloon keeper in the 1890s.

Continue north on Madison Street to **Silver Street**. Turn right on Silver Street, then right on **King Street**. Immediately on your left is a large, early-20th-century industrial building at **No. 42**. Originally built as a warehouse for the Buffalo, Rochester and Pittsburgh Railroad Company, this structure is located on the original site of Sts. Peter and Paul Catholic Church. Established in 1843 as the fourth Catholic parish in the city, and originally named St. Peter the Apostle Church, the congregation was home to a large German population who settled in the area. From the 1840s to 1910, the flourishing parish developed a campus here that included a church, school, rectory and convent. By the early 1900s, the congregation purchased a larger property at 720 West Main Street, and their King Street campus was sold to the railroad.

On the right, at the corner of King Street and Madison Park North, is the original site of School No. 2 (demolished in the mid-20th century), where Susan B. Anthony's sister Mary became the first female principal in the city school system. Also on the right, just past the park, is a diminutive Greek Revival-style house at the corner of King Street and Madison Park South.

This distinctive board-and-batten residence at **5 Madison Park South** is an unusual example of an early-19th-century vernacular design that has not been altered.

On your left, as you approach West Main Street, is **8 King Street**, one of the more interesting houses in the neighborhood. Built c. 1870 for Mayor Henry Fish, the brick, Second Empire-style house features dormer windows with round-headed hood moldings, cross motifs set in the brick of the tower wall, an elaborate chimney, and the original slate on the tower roof. Fish, the first Rochester mayor to be re-elected, serving from 1867-1869, also owned a canal boat business.

Take a right on West Main Street and continue several blocks. **The Church of Saints Peter and Paul** is on the right at **720 West Main Street**. Constructed during a one-and-a-half-year period from 1910 to 1911, the Lombard Romanesque-style church has a 145-foot bell tower modeled after the Cathedral of Lucca in Northern Italy. The church, with its red tile roof and inlays made of marble and stone, was designed by the Rochester firm of Gordon and Madden. The interior of the church follows the grand basilica form. Many of the interior elements were taken from the previous Saints Peter and Paul Church constructed in 1859 on King Street near the Susan B. Anthony House, and demolished in 1911. These include the 11 large windows, the High Altar, and the 10 statues around the apse. The church features a spectacular barrel-vaulted nave, with nine pairs of Corinthian columns, and an ivory-and-gold-embossed ceiling.

The intersection of West Main and Genesee streets, just past Saints Peter and Paul Church is known as Bull's Head, after The Bull's Head Tavern that flourished there in the 1850s, and a cattle market that was located there in the early 19th century.

To the left is **St. Mary's Hospital** at **89 Genesee Street**. St. Mary's was the first hospital established in the city, opening in 1857 under the direction of Mother Hieronymo of the Sisters of Charity. The first patients were seen in a group of old stone buildings formerly used as stables. Sick people were admitted without charge if they could not afford to pay. The hospital helped care for wounded and disabled soldiers during the Civil War, and at one point, temporary barracks were erected on the hospital lawn to accommodate soldiers.

Bear right on West Avenue (Route 33). On the left, overlooking the intersection, is the monumental **West Avenue Methodist Church**, at **51 Chili Avenue**. West Avenue Methodist was established by consolidating two smaller congregations to serve the growing population of the city's west side and neighboring suburbs. Constructed over an eight-year period between 1898 and 1906, the Richardsonian Romanesque-style church is built of randomly coursed, rock-faced Medina stone. The church features three octagonal turrets. The bell tower, which occupies one of the turrets, sits above a circular stained glass window.

Continue west on West Avenue, for many years one of the city's premier streets, lined with mansions of local businessmen and industrialists. You will approach the picturesque Danforth House on the right at **200 West Avenue**, built in 1848 by attorney Henry Danforth, whose family donated the house to the city in 1945 for a recreation center. Unique in the city, the house is one of the few remaining examples in the Rochester area of the type of Gothic cottage popularized by A. J. Downing in the 1840s. The steeply pitched gabled roof, pointed-arch windows, pierced balustrades and the small octagonal tower are characteristic elements of the style.

Canal Life

Take a right on Ames Street. Immediately on the left, on the northwest corner of Ames and West Avenue, was a notable industrial campus. From 1905 to the mid 1990s, it was dominated by the headquarters of Taylor Instrument Company, a pioneer Rochester firm established in 1849 to manufacturer thermometers. The former industrial complex on this site featured a massive brick building crowned by a large copper-clad dome.

Continue north on Ames Street and follow signs for Interstate 490 westbound. Turn left onto Interstate 490. Stay on Route 490 to Route 531. Take Route 531 to the exit for Route 259 (Union Street). Turn right and follow Route 259 into the village of Spencerport, located in the town of Ogden.

Ogden's first settler, George Warren Willey, moved to the area from East Haddam, Connecticut, in 1802, and lived close to today's Route 259 exit which leads into Spencerport. Indeed, the area just south of the exit was the heart of old Ogden.

With the construction of the Erie Canal a short two decades later, activity and settlement shifted north, nurturing and shaping both Spencerport and Brockport (which we will visit next), and elevating their fortunes when the canal was at its height of popularity.

Originally known as Spencer's Basin, Spencerport was laid out on a tract of land owned by William Spencer, who prospered from his fortunate acquisition of land through which the Erie Canal would be constructed. Spencer built the first sawmill in town and subdivided his property as demand for canal-side land increased. By the time the village was incorporated in 1832, the canal was carrying a rich stew of passengers and freight, while becoming a source of recreation for local residents. Author John T. Trowbridge, born in 1827, recalled an idyllic childhood of swimming in the canal in summer and skating on its frozen surface in winter. These canal pastimes continue well into the 20th century.

Continue north on Union Street and enter the village through a residential neighborhood which comprises a mix of late-19th- and early-20th-century architectural styles. The historic **Fairfield Cemetery**, on the right, was founded in 1853. Many of the village's earliest settlers, including members of the Spencer and Colby families, are buried there.

Spencerport Lift Bridge, Erie Canal   *Petronio*

Driving under the railroad tracks, continue north on Union Street. Upon entering the business district, note the unusual brick building on the left, at **147 Union Street**, on the corner of West Avenue. While the front of the building is contemporary, the tall, rear section was built in 1911 and originally housed the public library, a meeting room for the village board, the jail and the Spencerport Fire House. The unusual square tower on top of the building was used by the fire department to dry wet hoses after each fire. This building played the starring role in one of Spencerport's darkest days. On December 16, 1948, a massive fire ripped through the fire house itself, destroying most of the library's books, as well as the department's three fire engines. Damage was estimated at $75,000. The fire department has relocated to a modern building on Lyell Avenue.

Also on the left are two downtown anchors – the Colonial Revival-style **Etolian Lodge No. 479 F & AM Masonic Building** at **131 Union Street**, and the former Bank of Spencerport building at **No. 129**. The Neoclassical bank building, erected in 1925 and now a hardware store, is notable for its cast-stone facade, four Corinthian columns, and decorative cornice and entablature.

Take a left on Amity Street to see two historic churches and a well-maintained, 19th-century, residential neighborhood. On the right, the Romanesque Revival-style **First United Methodist Church** at **30 Amity Street** was built in 1870. The red brick church with a stone foundation has a tall spire and a large rose window with stained glass. Decorative corbeled gables and arched windows grace the church.

The 1915 **St. John the Evangelist Catholic Church** on the right, at **56 Amity Street**, is a monument to hard work and rocky fields. Designed by Pittsburgh architect John Comes and inspired by the Arts and Crafts movement, the unique building is constructed of brick and locally gathered fieldstones, and is topped by a slate roof and copper spire.

Take an immediate left on Martha Street. Take a right on West Avenue. On the left, at the intersection of West and Martha streets, is the second Gothic Revival house on this route. The board-and-batten-sided residence at **117 Martha Street** resembles the Danforth House in the city of Rochester. This picturesque frame house features a steeply pitched roof with six finials, and distinctive label hood moldings above the windows. Former resident Charles Upton made his fortune manufacturing the "Rochester Lamp," an innovative type of oil lamp.

West Avenue has long been considered one of the most elegant streets in Spencerport. On the right, opposite the Upton House, is a Queen Anne-style house with a decorative tower and large carriage barn at **72 West Avenue**.

Next door, the 1853 house at **78 West Avenue** features a finely detailed, late-19th-century porch, decorative windows, and a carriage barn. Also on the right, the eclectic house at **No. 112** combines a Second Empire tower topped with cast-iron cresting with Queen Anne-style cut work trim in the front gable.

As you drive along West Avenue, be sure to view the notable collection of late-19th-century carriage barns that survive in this attractive neighborhood.

Turn around at the end of West Avenue and return to Union Street. Then take a left turn and head toward the Erie Canal. The **Lift Bridge** traversing the canal opened in 1912. One of only 16 lift bridges along the entire canal route, this structure features a pony bedstead leg truss design, which is distinctive for its small scale and underground placement of counterweights.

As you cross the canal bridge, note the **Clyde Carter Memorial Gazebo** to the right, on the north side of the waterway. Constructed in 1995, it is named after a former mayor. The gazebo is located in **Towpath Park**, a major community beautification project also highlighted by a clock tower. The park provides docking, picnic tables, and access to the Erie Canal Heritage Trail. The trail is part of the state's Erie Canal Heritage Corridor program which brings attention to the corridor's unique cultural resources as an expression of New York State's heritage.

Continue north on Union Street to the intersection at the light. Turn left onto Canal Road, which parallels the canal and leads west to Adams Basin, a hamlet whose quiet today belies its activity during the 1800s. During the heyday of the Erie Canal, Adams Basin was bustling with factories, a boat yard, ice harvesting, a railroad, and dozens of farms in the area.

The center of Adams Basin, the intersection of Washington and Canal streets, is highlighted by the Queen Anne-style **United Methodist Church** (at **4292 Canal Road**), on the right.

Turn left on Washington Street and head south toward the canal. On the right, just before the canal bridge, is the historic **Canalside Inn** at **425 Washington Street**, which is listed in the National Register of Historic Places. Built in the early 1800s, this frame structure, with its attractive wraparound porch, was constructed in two stages. The Federal-style south section, facing the canal, was the first store in the area when Marcus Adams purchased the property in 1827. The Greek Revival-style north section of the house was added in 1858, complete with a full tavern to accommodate the abundant Erie Canal trade of the era.

Crossing over the canal, one again sees the Erie Canal Heritage Trail. Built in 1912, the **Washington Street Lift Bridge** is of the same truss design as its companion structure in Spencerport. Follow Washington Street south to Route 31. Turn right on Route 31 and continue west to Route 19.

Sell your farm

Soon after the Erie Canal arrived in the village of Brockport in 1823, attorney E.B. Holmes sent a flurry of letters to friends and family around the country. He encouraged them to move as quickly as possible to this prosperous place. He told one friend, a Vermont farmer, "Sell (your) farm for half price if (you) can ... there's no mistake about (it), come."

Today, the sumptuous architecture in Brockport's downtown area is testimony to the prosperity of this canal village in the 1800s. From 1823-1825, Brockport was the western terminus of the Erie Canal. As a result, the village became a center for shipping, which in turn, fueled the creation of hotels, saloons, and a variety of businesses that took advantage of the steady influx of people.

The canal opened six years after Connecticut-born builder Hiel Brockway began acquiring and selling property in what would become the village of Brockport. The naming of Brockport in November 1822 is one measure of Brockway's influence on village matters. According to one later account, Brockway so liked the idea of having the village named after him that he rewarded the founding fathers at his tavern as soon as the town meeting was over. "At the conclusion of the meeting, the crowd was handsomely refreshed."

At the intersection of Routes 31 and 19, you have reached the late-20th-century, commercial shopping district that has developed just south of Brockport. Turn right on Route 19 and drive north into the village.

As you approach the historic village, note the early-19th-century, Federal-style house constructed of Medina sandstone on the left, at **4617 Lake Road**. Now in the middle of a modern commercial area, this once-rural farmhouse was owned in the 1850s by Thomas Bascom, who had a bull and a team of oxen to till his acreage.

Continue north into the village. At the intersection of Main Street South and Park Avenue, the **Capen Hose Company**, on the right, at **237 Main Street South**, is the oldest fire station in the area in continuous use. Built in 1904, this village-designated landmark includes a firefighting museum with historic equipment from the 19th and early-20th centuries.

As you drive under the railroad bridge, you enter the village's historic residential area. Turn left onto College Street for a brief view of the **State University of New York College at Brockport**. On College Street, leading to the campus, you'll find a series of 19th-century houses. The house at **25 College Street**, on the left, was the home of the famous 19th-century novelist Mary Jane Holmes, author of more than 50 novels. Her house, known as the "Brown Cottage," drew tourists throughout her adult lifetime. Also on the left is **39 College Street**, an Italianate with off-center cupola built about 1870.

Located at the west end of College Street is the large campus of the State University College. The school's origins can be traced to 1834, when the Brockport Collegiate Institute was founded under the auspices of the Baptist Missionary Conference. The college changed names several times before becoming a part of the State University of New York system in 1948. Today, there are about 8,500 students at the school. Topped by a tower, the oldest and most prominent building on campus is the Neo-Georgian Hartwell Hall, built in 1941.

Morgan-Manning House   *Padelt*

Turn around and return to Main Street and take a left. An especially important Brockport landmark is the **Morgan-Manning House** on the right, at **151 Main Street South**. Located on the corner of South Street, it was built by John C. Ostrom in 1854, and became best known as the home of the Morgan family, whose members lived there from 1867 to 1964. Patriarch Dayton S. Morgan was best known for manufacturing the McCormick reaper with his partner William H. Seymour. The house is built in the Tuscan villa style, with a low hipped roof, broad eaves, and a well-proportioned cupola. Decorative and unusally massive columns, along with elaborate woodwork, adorn the front porch. Listed in the National Register of Historic Places, the house serves as headquarters for the Western Monroe Historical Society and is open to the public. Sara Morgan Manning, who died in a fire at the house in 1964 when she was 96, was married in the mansion on December 19, 1893. Guests were driven in sleighs to the house, where a six-piece orchestra played, surrounded by bouquets of buttercups and roses.

Across the street from the Morgan-Manning House is the **Nativity of the Blessed Virgin Mary Catholic Church** at **152 Main Street South**. Built in 1927, this stone edifice is a striking example of early-20th-century Gothic Revival design.

Continue north to the intersection of Main and State streets. This marks the gateway to the village's historic business district, which extends for three blocks between State Street and the Erie Canal. This village-designated historic district, a concentration of 45 commercial buildings, contains the most intact collection of Victorian-era, village commercial architecture in Monroe County. It also is a testimony to contemporary good sense. Unlike other communities, Brockport residents rejected a proposed Urban Renewal Plan in 1965 that would have resulted in the destruction of many historic buildings.

Although one can drive through and observe the district, walking is recommended due to the large concentration of buildings worth viewing. Nearby are several municipal parking lots.

At the intersection of Main and State streets, you can see four of the village's historic church buildings. On the left, at **124 Main Street South**, is the Gothic Revival-style **First Baptist Church**, built in 1863-64 and enlarged in 1926.

Also on the left, at the corner of Erie Street, is the **United Methodist Church** at **92 Main Street South**. Built in 1876, this imposing brick building was designed by noted Rochester architect, Andrew J. Warner. Villagers fought against construction of this church, arguing that the church would stop commercial Main Street from expanding any farther south if it was built on that corner lot. Indeed, the growth of downtown's commercial district was stopped by the construction of the church. This Romanesque Revival-style church has been compared to a European castle, with its two flanking asymmetrical towers and steeply pitched hipped roofs. Stone and brick are used to vary the texture of the building, which includes elaborate corbeled brick work. The large doors on the east facade were installed in 1991. They weigh 250 pounds and were constructed by local cabinetmaker John Deats. The four-faced clock in the south tower was added to the church in 1914.

Another village landmark is **St. Luke's Episcopal Church**, **97 Main Street South**, on the right. Located here on the corner of Main and State streets since 1855, the church is an outstanding example of late-19th-century Gothic Revival design, with its Medina sandstone walls, limestone trim, and rich collection of stained glass windows, including several by the Tiffany Studios in New York City. Expanded in 1882-84 and 1903, with the construction of the adjacent parish house, the church is listed in the National Register of Historic Places.

Take a right turn on State Street for a brief view of two prominent, 19th-century village buildings. **The First Presbyterian Church**, on the left, at **35 State Street**, is an outstanding example of Greek Revival-style religious architecture, as characterized by its massive Corinthian columns and elaborate cornice. Of brick construction with stone details, this 1855 building also is listed in the National Register of Historic Places.

For more historical information about Brockport, visit the **Seymour Building**, now the Village of Brockport Municipal Building, also on the left, at **49 State Street**. Built in 1843, the three-story building was remodeled in the Second Empire style in 1865. The house was donated to the community in the 1930s by the family of William Seymour, a partner in the firm of Seymour and Morgan, which successfully manufactured the McCormick reaper. Today, the upper floors of the Seymour Building feature the **Emily Knapp Local History Museum and Library**. Among the many items here are a pioneer kitchen, a children's toy and game room, and a sideboard once owned by Hiel Brockway.

Turn around and return to Main Street and take a right to begin your exploration of the village's historic business district. Immediately on the right, at the corner of Main and State streets, is a contemporary landmark at **89-93 Main Street South**. The **Strand Theatre** would be distinctive in any community, but its Streamlined Moderne-style facade is particularly prominent in historic Brockport. Built in 1907, the building, originally known as the Winslow Block, was comprised of retail shops on the first floor, and later, a second-floor theater. When it first opened in 1916, the "Lyric Threatre" charged 10 cents admission. Movie-goers of this early era could visit the first floor "Palace of Sweets" after the show. An early 1900s newspaper article praised the Revelas brothers, owners of the sweet shop: "With their famous 'Banana Split' they have comforted many a school girl subsisting on boarding house fare."

Renamed the Strand Theatre in the 1920s, the building was extensively remodeled in 1946 to its present appearance, with the theater occupying the entire structure. Today the Strand glitters with red, dark blue, and black Carrara glass.

Across the street, to the left, the three-story commercial building, built in 1871-1872 at **84-86 Main Street South**, includes two historic storefronts with the original cast-iron columns manufactured by the W. H. Cheney firm in Rochester. Round-arch windows with curved stone lintels mark the third story, while an attractive cornice above is adorned with eight elaborately carved brackets. The building was constructed on property that belonged to E. B. Holmes, the attorney who encouraged everyone he knew to move to Brockport in 1833. Holmes, the son-in-law of village founder Hiel Brockway, lived with his family in a large brick house with a shaded garden that formerly stood on this property.

Also on the left, at the corner of King Street, is the prominent bank at **66 Main Street South**. This sophisticated Neoclassical building from 1927 is notable for its cut-stone facade that is punctuated by a bronze entrance and large round-arch windows.

Across the street, at **67-71 Main Street South**, is the Masonic Temple Building, an outstanding example of early-20th-century, Neoclassical commercial architecture in the village. Built in 1916, it replaced the "Gleason Block," the previous commercial building on this site that was destroyed in a spectacular fire on November 21, 1915.

The increasingly elaborate buildings along Main Street reflect the prosperity of Brockport in the late 1800s. Though the village remained small, its national influence increased dramatically when Morgan and Seymour made the village the first place in the country to successfully mass-produce Cyrus McCormick's celebrated reaper in 1846. The reaper enabled farmers to skip many laborious steps in the harvesting process, revolutionizing their jobs by allowing them to use a machine to help harvest their crops. By the 1870s, the village had become a flourishing manufacturing center for farming equipment. The Johnston Harvester Company, established in 1870 by Samuel Johnson, grew to be one of the largest manufacturers in Monroe County.

The sudden rise to prosperity is exemplified by a comment from one newspaper editor in 1870, who described some of the village's older buildings as "lean or sagging in center or at corners." "Let us brush up Main Street, and perhaps business will be livelier," the editor implored.

The colorful and attractive **Decker Block** at **39-41 Main Street South** on the right, constructed in 1871, answered the editor's call. This High Victorian-style, three-story corner block is the most elaborately designed commercial building in the business district. The contrasting red brick walls and gray stone trim create an attractive polychrome effect. Other features include round-arch windows and stone lintels, cast-iron columns, a dentiled cornice and extensive cut-stone detailing. Constructed by J. D. Decker, a Brockport attorney, the building originally included a bank on the first floor and professional offices on the second floor. The entire third floor is an auditorium that once served as the community's primary concert hall and ballroom. Even the plain north side of the Decker Building holds a special place in Brockport lore. Best seen on foot, the large painted advertisement for Ivory Soap is a rare example of advertising art. Created some time before 1930, the sign was repainted in 1993.

Take a right at Market Street. Here, a series of distinctive commercial buildings on the left was built following a disastrous fire on January 12, 1877, that leveled the block from 5 to 27 Market Street. The fire, caused by an oil lamp that dropped to the floor inside the former Methodist church, caused widespread damage to the primarily wood frame structures of the era. Their replacements are brick, which was considered to be more fireproof. The buildings at **5-7-9 Market Street** (1883) and **11-13** (1877) are attractive structures with decorative features, marking them as products of a prosperous time.

One of the most distinctive commercial buildings in the district is the finely crafted brick, two-story building across the street at **14 Market Street**. This notable structure, built c. 1881-1902, features a facade with some of the most elaborate decorative brick and terra cotta detailing to be seen in the downtown historic district.

One of the finest of the buildings constructed after the fire is the three-story brick commercial structure on the left at **19-25 Market Street**, built from 1881-1889. This building, with the elaborate brick detailing, includes a "little brother" two-story wing on the west side. The horizontal band of decorative brick between each window is made up of bricks angled to expose their corners. Eight cast-iron columns flank each of the four front doorways. The first business to occupy the building, the Guelf Seed Store, sold flower seeds and bulbs and distributed catalogues throughout the country.

Turn around and return to Main Street and turn right. As you approach the canal, street names such as "Water Street" and "Clinton Street" recall the early history of this renowned waterway, the single most important public works project ever built in the United States. New York State Governor DeWitt Clinton, whose vigilant efforts spurred the construction of the Erie Canal, is recognized with a street named in his honor.

Some of the most attractive buildings in the village, dating from the early-19th century, are located here. A three-story, masonry building at **22-24 Main Street South**, on the left, was constructed between the 1820s and 1834 and enlarged during the 1860s and 1870s. Once a common sight, this is one of the few Greek Revival, cut-stone storefronts still in existence. Located on the corner of Main and Clinton streets, the building features seven square, cut-stone columns with Doric capitals and a projecting wood cornice. The petite barber pole marks a place where hair has been trimmed and tamed since at least 1875. Inside, decorative pressed metal sheathing remains on the walls and ceiling.

Decker Building   *Petronio*

Also on the left, at **14, Main Street South**, is the brick **United States Post Office**, with its spacious windows, cut-stone pilasters and simple Doric capitals. Built in 1940, the Post Office was constructed during a massive, government-financed building effort following the Great Depression of 1929, and was one of 40,000 public buildings erected during the era. Its style has been called "Starved Classical," inspired by classical architecture, but without dramatic elements such as porticos and columns. "Starved Classical" buildings are said to fit with the emphasis on simplicity and thrift during the administration of President Franklin Delano Roosevelt, architect of the New Deal.

Across the street, a row of brick buildings includes some of the earliest surviving commercial architecture in the village. Since its construction in 1834-1847, with some remodeling later in the 19th century, the brick and stone building on the right, at **13-15 Main Street South**, has anchored the block.

Although the canal no longer serves as the commercial pulse of the village, the 1867-1868 commercial building at **1 Main Street South**, on the right, presides with quiet elegance over the historic waterway and Main Street. The building was one of seven toll stations on the Erie Canal, and boasts one of the most highly decorated commercial facades in the village, complete with elaborate cast-iron details, such as the original projecting cornice above the storefront. The building is the only surviving 19th-century commercial structure in the village that uses its ground-floor level next to the canal for commercial space. During the 19th century, canal shipping was conducted at the ground-floor level, using warehouses, docks and basins along the banks.

The adjacent **Main Street Lift Bridge** over the canal was constructed in 1915 as part of a massive New York state project that enlarged the Erie Canal and the feeder canals serving the state. This 131-foot-long, single-span lift bridge is one of five similar lift bridges in Monroe County. The bridge is architecturally significant because of the location of the counterweights below the level of the deck. Typically, counterweights are located in the towers over each end of a bridge. The lift tower (1913) is the only concrete canal tower in Monroe County, and one of only four concrete bridge towers along the canal.

To travel to Clarkson, cross the canal bridge and follow Main Street (Route 19) north to the intersection of East Avenue, the village line. Here, Route 19 becomes Lake Road as you enter the town of Clarkson.

Clarkson

Clarkson's abundance of Federal and Greek Revival-style houses are evidence of the longevity of this small town. Settlers began moving to the town of Clarkson between 1800 and 1804. Clarkson Corners, a thriving hamlet at the inter-section of Lake and Ridge roads, became a center of commerce before the Erie Canal spurred the growth of other settlements in Western New York.

Though the Canal's success enabled Brockport to overshadow Clarkson in size, Clarkson remained an important 19th-century center for farming and brick-making. Clarkson taverns served Ridge Road travelers.

Continue north on Route 19 (Lake Road) where an important collection of early-19th-century residential architecture is located. In 1994, much of the hamlet was designated the Clarkson Corners Historic District and listed in the National Register of Historic Places.

An important, early-20th-century property is located on the left at **3845 Lake Road** behind the tall hedge that lines the roadway. Built in 1906, this 40-room, Georgian Revival mansion was the home of Fred H. Gordon, a local boy who achieved significant business success as director of the Lincoln Alliance Bank and co-owner of a coal company. Originally called "Whitehall," this gentleman's farm was known for the prize Guernsey cattle and pheasants that Gordon raised here.

One of the finest Federal-style brick houses in the area is the Simeon B. Jewett House, on the left, at **3779 Lake Road**. Built in 1828, the house is distinguished for its finely detailed entrance. Other characteristic Federal elements include twelve-over-twelve, double-hung sash windows with delicate muntins.

Another attractive Federal-style entryway with an elaborate fanlight and sidelights, is next door at **3773 Lake Road**, the Henry Martyn House, built in the 1820s. The classical porch and other bracketed details are later additions.

The David Lee House, on the left at **3749 Lake Road**, is a Greek Revival residence built in 1840, which is notable for its circular window in the pediment. Its window panes are larger than those found in the earlier Federal houses, due to the greater availability of glass by 1840. The front entrance has a decorative, carved paneled door, and the side porch has square columns incised with Greek designs.

The story of the failed romance linked to the Greek Revival mansion next door at **3741 Lake Road** has proved to be almost as durable as the Corinthian columns gracing the entranceway. One of the principal architectural monuments of Clarkson, the distinctive mansion was built in 1850 by John Bowman as a wedding present for his fiancee, Kate Bellinger. As Bellinger waited for her wedding day, Bowman had a change of heart and planned his escape. He disappeared from town before the two were married, never to return. Bellinger spent the rest of her life in Clarkson, wearing the black clothing of mourning. The relatively late construction date for this style is suggested by the richness and complexity of the design. The house is distinguished by an imposing portico with Corinthian columns, and the facade and a smaller portico with Doric columns on the north elevation. The surmounting cupola with pediments on all sides is an uncommon element in Greek Revival design.

The historic center of the hamlet of Clarkson is located at the intersection of Lake Road (State Route 19) and Ridge Road West (Route 104). To the left, near the corner of Lake and Ridge roads, is the house of one of Clarkson's most famous sons, attorney Henry R. Selden, at **8396 Ridge Road**. Selden defended Susan B. Anthony when she was charged with voting illegally and fined $100. In the 1850s, Selden achieved statewide prominence as a founder of the New York State Republican party. From 1857-58 he served as the state's first Republican Lieutenant Governor, and in the 1860s was appointed Associate Justice of the New York State Court of Appeals. Selden's son George also was notable as the creator of the first combustion engine for automobiles in 1877 — years before Henry Ford made a fortune as the popularly acknowledged father of American automobiles.

Turn right on Ridge Road and drive east to see the historic Village Green in front of the **Clarkson Community Church**. Most of the essential elements of 19th-century life were once found surrounding the Village Green: a church, a school, stables and a shop. Church and school buildings survive. Built in 1825, the Clarkson Community Church (a former Congregational church) on the right, at **8339 Ridge Road West**, has long been a significant visual landmark on Ridge Road. One of the oldest surviving churches in the county, it reflects the New England architectural influences which touched western New York as a result of migration from the eastern seaboard. Architecturally, the church illustrates the prevailing Federal form and detailing (pilasters, pediment, entablature and fan window) combined with an influence of the Italianate style in the round-arch windows that were updated when the church was remodeled in the 1860s. The facade has remained virtually unchanged since the spire was added in the 1890s.

Next door, the Clarkson Academy, **8343 Ridge Road West**, was built in 1853 of locally manufactured brick. One of the few surviving 19th-century academy buildings in the area, this handsome Greek Revival structure presents a statement of classical proportion and detailing, with wide brick pilasters, a triangular pediment, and an octangonal bell tower. Like the adjacent church, it presents an important example of outstanding 19th-century public architecture.

Clarkson's Village Green and Community Church   *Padelt*

Another notable Federal residence is the Albert Palmer House on the right at **8251 Ridge Road West**. Built in the 1820s, the house has flush boards on the facade and beveled siding on the sides and rear. The elegant entrance features a fanlight with delicate metalwork and an unusual sculpted cornice supported on fluted and curved brackets.

The Clarkson hamlet and its outstanding collection of well-preserved historic buildings end here. To return to Rochester, continue east on Ridge Road West (Route 104). Take the first right, Sweden Walker Road (Route 260), and proceed south to the intersection of Brockport-Spencerport Road (Route 31). Go left on Route 31.

You may return quickly to Rochester via Routes 531 and 490, or you can take an optional short detour through Northampton Park and the heart of old Ogden on a rural route where farms, historic homes, and parkland quietly coexist. To pursue this option, from Route 31, take the second right onto Hubbell Road to enter North-hampton Park, named for the original Monroe County town established west of the Genesee River in 1797. Drive south until the road intersects with Colby Street. Take a left on Colby.

Immediately on the left is **Springdale Farm at 696 Colby Street**. First established as the Amos Niles farm in the early 1800s, it features a large stone house with a mansard roof and pedimented dormer windows. The residence was reportedly built in two phases, with the lower floors constructed in the early 1800s and the upper floor with its mansard roof built around the 1880s. Today, Springdale Farm is part of a farm complex that is open to the public. Turkeys, peacocks, chickens, sheep and horses are among the animals at the farm, which also includes a playground and picnic area. Established in 1975 by Monroe County, the farm is now operated by Heritage Christian Homes Inc.

Also on the left, at **568 Colby Street**, is the former Eastman Colby Homestead, a two-story, wood frame house built in 1811. Colby moved to the town of Ogden in 1804 with his parents and a sister. They joined four brothers who previously had moved to the area. The house now serves as the **Ogden Historical Society Museum** and is open to the public. It features wide ash floors, two back-to-back fireplaces on the first floor, and a six-foot-square chimney. A third fireplace is in an upstairs master bedroom.

The peculiar structure that looks like a stranded lighthouse behind the house is actually the 1915 Bridge Tender's House and Terminal Building from the Erie Canal in Spencerport.

At the intersection of Washington Street (Route 36), continue east on **Colby Street**. Farther along, at **No. 345** on the right, is a residence built in 1825 by Dr. John Webster, the first physician in the town of Ogden. Webster arrived in 1805, living first in a log cabin. The house was reportedly a station on the Underground Railroad when the doctor's son, Alvin, worked the farm and promoted the abolition of slavery. The two-story house was constructed of bricks made on a farm north of Adams Basin.

The intersection of Colby and Union streets (Route 259) marks the end of the tour. To return to Rochester, take a left on Route 259 and an immediate right on Route 531, which then leads to Route 490 east.

Bridge Tender's House   *Petronio*

Pittsford and Mendon:
The Early Towns

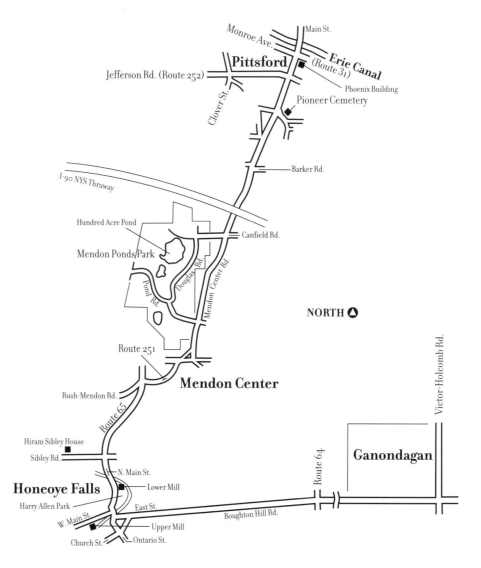

Main St.

Monroe Ave.

Pittsford

Erie Canal
(Route 31)

Jefferson Rd. (Route 252)

Phoenix Building

Pioneer Cemetery

Clover St.

Barker Rd.

I-90 NYS Thruway

Hundred Acre Pond

Canfield Rd.

Mendon Ponds Park

Douglas Rd.

Mendon Center Rd.

Pond Rd.

NORTH ▲

Route 251

Mendon Center

Rush-Mendon Rd.

Route 65

Victor-Holcomb Rd.

Hiram Sibley House

Sibley Rd.

Ganondagan

N. Main St.

Honeoye Falls

Lower Mill

Route 64

Harry Allen Park

East St.

Boughton Hill Rd.

W. Main St.

Upper Mill

Church St.

Ontario St.

The Upper Mill, Honeoye Falls   *Padelt*

This tour begins on North Main Street in the village of Pittsford and proceeds south to Honeoye Falls.

Mileage: Approximately 16 miles, not including optional detour to Ganondagan.

Time: Approximately 1½ hours

~ Open to the Public ~

The Little House
18 Monroe Avenue, Pittsford
phone 381-2941

Town of Mendon Historical Society
1 Allen Park Drive, Honeoye Falls
phone 624-5660

Writer Arch Merrill called Pittsford "the Mother of Monroe," because the town had the first school, the first library, and the first doctor in Monroe County. "She was a thriving settlement when Rochester was a miasmic mudhole," he wrote in 1945.

Our route through the county's oldest community leads from Pittsford village through the town of Pittsford and into the town of Mendon. It is a route marked by architectural hybrids, such as a cobblestone house with a brick addition; and by the often striking juxtaposition of old houses and open space with new developments, which recently have become abundant in this part of the county. The tour ends in historic Honeoye Falls, a village featuring decorative Queen Anne-style houses, landmark churches, and massive stone mill buildings on the banks of Honeoye Creek.

Thirteen Thousand Acres

The present-day village of Pittsford sits on a limestone dome through which flows an underground spring. It was long a gathering place for the Seneca Indians. The "Big Spring" also attracted the area's earliest white settlers. Among the first were cousins Simon and Israel Stone from Washington County, New York. In 1789, the cousins purchased a huge tract of land, 13,296 acres, encompassing all of Pittsford and Perinton, for about 36 cents an acre from land speculators Oliver Phelps and Nathaniel Gorham. Israel Stone built the first log cabin in town at the Big Spring, where 38 State Street stands today. His cousin lived nearby in a cabin at the corner of South and Locust streets, and established the town's first flour mill in 1791 southeast of the village.

The early settlement was the center of the town of Northfield, established as part of Ontario County in 1792. Northfield included most of present-day Monroe County east of the Genesee River. As more settlers were drawn to the area, new towns were established. Thus in 1808, Northfield became Boyle, which in turn became Smallwood in 1813. In 1814, Smallwood was divided into two towns, Brighton (see Chapter 1) and Pittsford.

Pittsford was named by a war veteran as his reward for heroic service in the War of 1812. Colonel Caleb Hopkins, who moved here in the 1790s, named the town after his hometown of Pittsford, Vermont. Hopkins was promoted to Brevet Brigadier General in 1816 and died two years later at age 47. He is buried in Pittsford's Pioneer Burying Ground, which is discussed later in the tour.

As befitting the "Mother of Monroe," Pittsford has maintained and cultivated its history. As Arch Merrill observed, Pittsford "has remained unsullied, immaculate and herself." The village resembles main streets of an earlier era with its carefully preserved storefronts. This is in part the result of an assertive effort within the community led by Historic Pittsford, a private, not-for-profit preservation advocacy group, and the village's Architectural and Preservation Review Board.

One-third of the village is listed in the National Register of Historic Places, and the entire village is a locally designated preservation district. Property owners are required to seek approval of any changes to visible architectural features of their buildings, ensuring that the character of the house and of the village is retained.

This tour begins on North Main Street, just beyond Schoen Place, across the bridge on the south side of the Erie Canal, and north of the Four Corners intersection of Main and State streets. If you can walk around the village on this first part of the tour, you will see more, and be less likely to cause a traffic jam on busy Main Street. An informative walking tour brochure is available at the **Village Hall** at **21 North Main Street**, and at Historic Pittsford's headquarters in the 1819 "**Little House**" at **18 Monroe Avenue**, just west of the Four Corners next to the fire department. This diminutive former law office is open to the public.

We begin at the **Port of Pittsford Park**, located on the south side of the canal, opposite Schoen Place and on the east side of North Main Street. Now a popular site for picnic lunches and summer concerts, the port originally was constructed as part of New York State's 1911-1912 canal enlargement project and became an important coaling station for canal tugboats.

Opposite the park, on the west side of Main Street, is the brick 1887 Eastlake-style Agate-Zornow house, at **27 North Main Street**, designed by the Rochester architectural firm of Otis and

Crandall. Built by the owner of a flour mill and malt house in Schoen Place, the house illustrates the prosperity derived from the canal businesses in the late 19th century.

Two doors south at **21 North Main Street** is the **Wiltsie Memorial Building**, housing the offices of the Village of Pittsford. In 1937, Mary Wiltsie Field donated this fine brick Colonial Revival building to the village.

The centerpiece of the village is the Phoenix Building, at **4 South Main Street**, which has overlooked the village crossroads since its construction as a hotel in 1824. An earlier tavern was located on the site from 1807 to serve stagecoach trade. This distinguished Federal building features stepped gables, a gable fanlight, and an arcade of elliptical-arch recesses on the first floor.

Among the illustrious hotel guests were the Marquis de Lafayette, DeWitt Clinton, Daniel Webster, and Cornelius Vanderbilt. In the mid-20th century, a gas station was erected obstructing the north facade, and eventually, after a fire, the building became vacant. In 1964, the late publisher Andrew D. Wolfe purchased the building, rehabilitated it for office use, and restored many of its exterior features that had been lost, including the small grass lawn facing the village's Four Corners. His efforts helped launch Historic Pittsford.

Pittsford's commercial district contains a number of distinctive 19th-century buildings. Across the street from the Phoenix Building, at the north and southwest corners of Monroe Avenue and Main Street, are two notable examples, both former general stores built at opposite ends of the century.

The three-story, painted brick Parker Block at **3-5 South Main Street** was built c. 1826 as the village's first general store, and is considered one of the finest early commercial structures remaining in the region. At the other corner is the Queen Anne-style 1886 former Wiltsie and Crump Block, which features Medina sandstone lintels and sills and decorative brickwork above its second-story windows.

Moving south on Main Street, you'll see the c. 1890 **Town Hall**, at **11 South Main Street**, another Queen Anne-style, late-19th-century structure, with an elaborate mix of wall textures made of Medina sandstone, brick, terra cotta, wood and slate.

Phoenix Building   *Padelt*

133

The buildings at **15-17** and **25 South Main Street** are Federal-style, former residences adapted for commercial use. Notice the elevated first floors, which are characteristic of the style.

The building at **23 South Main Street,** now occupied by **Hicks and McCarthy's,** originally was built about 1850 and served as the church of the newly organized Christ Church Episcopal. Around the turn of the century, after the church moved to its present location, the structure was adapted to its present use as a restaurant, and the commercial store front with its Neoclassical cornice was added.

The present **Christ Church Episcopal** stands at **36 South Main Street**, on the corner of Locust Street. The handsome Medina sandstone structure was designed by the prominent Rochester architect Andrew J. Warner (see sidebar, Chapter 2). Built in 1869, the Gothic Revival-style edifice features a square tower whose Seth Thomas clock has faces on all four sides. Although the clock now is electrified, it originally was wound by hand.

On the other corner of Locust Street, at **44 South Main Street**, is the elaborate Vogt-Allen House built around 1894. The multiple gables and extensive and decorative woodwork in the gables and on the turreted wraparound porch are hallmarks of the Queen Anne style.

Continue south on Main Street to the Elliott-Hargous House, located on the left at **52-54 South Main Street**, and owned by the St. Louis Roman Catholic Church. The house is considered one of the most important Federal-style houses in Monroe County, but has a sad early history. Prosperous distiller Augustus Elliott constructed the building for his intended bride Jane Penfield, of the family for which the town of Penfield was named. The beautiful house was not enough, however, to induce Penfield to marry Elliott. Elliott is said to have killed himself when she rejected him.

The graceful and elegant brick house, built between 1810 and 1814, features stepped gables, each incorporating two chimneys. The large entrance, with its unusual elliptical fanlight and sidelights, is distinctive. The bricks came from the Elihu Doud brickyard south of the village in Lusk's Hollow. The Hargous family, later owners, were New Yorkers who used the residence as a country house and were known for their entertaining during the Civil War.

The rough-hewn stone entrance to **Stonegate Lane**, across the street, marks the original spot where Augustus Elliott operated his distillery and ashery – a facility for making potash and other substances from ashes in the early 1800s. The stone entrance was built in 1902 and led to the Eugene Satterlee House, a 1902 Dutch Colonial house, now on Sutherland Street. The name of the estate, "Hyllgarth," meaning "garden on the hill," is still stamped on the metal sign. The residences along the lane today were built in the 1930s and 1940s.

On the right, set back just before the major intersection of Main Street and Jefferson Road, is **77 South Main Street**, a charming and picturesque house built about 1855. This diminutive Gothic Revival residence has rich exterior woodwork that includes serrated verge boards along most of the roof eaves, as well as scrollwork brackets and finely turned balusters and posts on the porch.

Continuing on Main Street, outside the village, is a fine example of the Italianate-style former farmhouse on the right at **169 South Main Street**. Characteristic of this style is the hipped roof topped with a cupola, complete with round-

44 South Main Street   *Olenick*

arched windows and a finial, bracketed wide eaves, and porches with chamfered posts and decorative brackets.

The historic nucleus of Pittsford is located at the intersection of South Main Street, Mendon Road, and Mendon Center Road. Bear left at the light and drive past the Pioneer Cemetery. Turn left into the parking lot next to the old brick Mile Post Schoolhouse. This is the best place to see the school, as well as the stately Lusk farmhouse across the intersection at 1 Mendon Center Road.

The first schoolhouse in Monroe County was built on this site in 1794. It was a one-room log building that served the entire area for 10 years. Local students paid $1.50 to the teacher for each 13-week term. Among the students who attended this school in the early period was Titus Lord, a 14- or 15-year-old slave bought by Colonel Caleb Hopkins in Canandaigua in 1813. In 1857, the present brick one-room schoolhouse was erected as **District No. 1 School**, and was used as a school until 1944, when the Pittsford school system was centralized. Today, the building serves as a community meeting hall.

Pioneer Burying Ground

The **Pioneer Burying Ground**, adjacent to the schoolhouse, is the final home of many of early Pittsford's most prominent citizens. Among them are 18 Revolutionary War veterans and eight veterans of the War of 1812. Other luminaries include Dr. John Ray, Northfield's first doctor and first town clerk; and Silas Nye, the first supervisor of Northfield.

Looking out from the parking lot to the far corner is a clear view of the Lusk farmhouse at **1 Mendon Center Road**. Since its purchase in 1806, more than seven generations of the Lusk family have operated the farm. In 1992, the adjacent farmland was sold for development, but the gracious painted brick house was preserved and still presides over the area. Built in 1822, the house is a fine example of the Federal style and features a fan in the gable and over the door. Around 1850, the Greek Revival porch with paneled square posts was added.

Continue the tour by taking a left onto Mendon Center Road, which runs past the Lusk farm-house. Upon reaching the top of the hill, just beyond the Calkins Road intersection, the town's scenic farmlands come into view. One of Pittsford's most distinguished, well-preserved historic farms is located at **219 Mendon Center Road**, on the right, and across the road at No. 230. Known as the Barker-Knickerbocker farm, the property was acquired by William H. Barker in 1860. In 1883, he built the handsome Italianate farmhouse located at No. 219, which replaced an earlier farmhouse, parts of which have been incorporated in the existing former horse barn located closest to the road. The house at **No. 230** was built in the 1890s for William Barker's son. The Knickerbocker family continues to maintain both properties, with their fine barns and out-buildings. Development rights of the surrounding farmland were sold to the town of Pittsford as a means to preserve open space and continue the agricultural use of the land.

At the top of the hill, on the right, at **311 Mendon Center Road**, is a pleasant Greek Revival house, built around 1825. The rear section of the house dates from 1795, and was the first frame house in Pittsford. The five-bay, one-and-a-half story main portion features frieze windows, a hip roof, and an attractive Greek Revival porch that combines round fluted columns with

Pioneer Burying Ground   *Petronio*

square ones. The tall, board-and-batten barn on the property also is significant. Built around 1892, this gambrel roof barn is an early example of a Wells truss barn. The Wells truss frame was patented by John Talcott Wells of Scottsville and was a creative advance in barn construction. The framing system was noted for its efficient use of wood and for providing huge open spaces for better movement and storage of hay. Curved, laminated trusses were constructed by bending, bolting, and spiking planks, which left the interior free from posts. Most Wells truss barns are found within 90 miles of Scottsville and usually can be identified by the "lazy W" molding over the window in the upper gable end of the barn.

Located in a valley on the left, at **476 Mendon Center Road**, is an attractive cobblestone residence, built around 1830, with a side brick addition constructed sometime in the late 1800s. The picturesque grounds include agricultural outbuildings and mature trees, which recall the town's rural past. The expansion of the house reflects the changing needs of its original owners, David and Sarah Acer, who had seven children. For a time, their granddaughters also lived there, and their son John lived next door as an adult with his five children and eight servants.

Cobblestone Architecture

About 90 percent of all cobblestone buildings in the United States are located within a 70-mile radius of Rochester. Of the more than 600 cobblestone structures in western New York, over 105 are located in Monroe County. Their very existence here can be attributed to three factors. Forty thousand years ago, cobble-sized stones were deposited by the retreating Ice-Age glacier, which scattered them widely or deposited them in masses or moraines. Streams flowing through the glacier and water action in Lake Ontario abraded and washed the stones into smooth, rounded cobbles. The second factor is the existence of limestone found in area rocks that was used to make mortar. The third factor was the men who built cobblestone structures. There was an abundance of masons in the area who came here to work on the Erie Canal in the early years of the 19th century, and during its enlargement between 1832 and 1862. These masons were experts at formulating the limestone mortar and also were looking for work. Most cobblestone buildings were built between 1825 and 1860.

Most cobblestone structures in western New York are residential buildings, but there are others, like the Chili Cobblestone School (see chapter 3), that were built as schoolhouses, churches, barns, blacksmith shops, and other commercial structures.

Construction techniques vary, but most buildings have block-stone quoins as corner supports and rows of cobblestones, separated by mortar. Facades usually are more sophisticated than the sides and rear. Stones often were selected and arranged by color, size, shape, and orientation. One of the most decorative patterns is the herringbone, in which one row of elongated stones is slanted one way, and the next row is slanted the other way. Mortar joints and color also vary widely, which is why cobblestone restoration often is a challenge.

Cobblestone detail   *Petronio*

Indian Trails

We enter the town of Mendon soon after crossing under the New York State Thruway, a transition also marked by the increasing abundance of horse farms. Early settlers arrived in Mendon in the first years of the 1790s, drawn by rushing creeks, waterfalls, and fertile land. Zebulon Norton purchased 1,820 acres from Phelps and Gorham in 1791 and established a grist and saw mill on the west bank of Honeoye Creek in what today is Honeoye Falls. By 1830, mills were so successful in the area that there were dozens of them along the banks of Honeoye Creek.

Originally part of Bloomfield in Ontario County, the town of Mendon was established in 1812. The town's name may have come from Mendon, Massachusetts, where pioneer settlers Caleb Taft and Josiah Fish originated. Another early resident was Brigham Young, who lived in Mendon briefly as a young man before joining Joseph Smith's religious group and leading the Mormons to Utah.

Mendon Ponds Park is a pleasant detour, allowing you to view a cobblestone house, a swimming pond, and many picnic areas. Turn right onto Canfield Road, the first entrance to Mendon Ponds Park. Established in 1928, it is the largest Monroe County Park and is nationally known for its display of glacial topography. Long ago, the park was an important hunting and fishing site for the Seneca Indians. Among the original Indian trails in the park is the scenic path around the Mendon Ponds. Southwest of the park was the second largest known Seneca village called "Totiakton."

Turn left on **Douglas Road**. The cobblestone farmhouse on the right at **No. 10** is now owned by the County of Monroe. Built in the early 1830s by Jeremiah Stewart, the house features multicolored fieldstones, which are laid up four rows to each gray limestone quoin at the corners. The house also displays Greek Revival elements, especially in the handsome porch with fluted Doric columns. This farmhouse is one of 10 cobblestone buildings in the town of Mendon, and one of seven in the town listed in the National Register of Historic Places.

Continue exploring the park by car or by foot, or return to Mendon Center Road via Canfield Road and turn right to continue south.

The Eastlake-style farmhouse on the left at **822 Mendon Center Road** rests on property that was owned by the same family from 1852 to 1974. To get a closer look, turn left onto Topspin Drive and park. Built on a 230-acre farm in 1888 by David Smith, the house replaced an earlier farm-house on the land he had purchased in 1852. The house's typical Eastlake-style features include an asymmetrical plan, as well as balconies, bay windows, and machine-made decorative wood detailing on the porches and in the gables. Contributing to the historic setting are several preserved outbuildings.

Return to Mendon Center Road and turn left. The two-story, wood frame Federal house on the right at **833 Mendon Center Road** is one of the oldest on the route, and was built in at least two stages. The rear saltbox part of the house was erected before 1820. The main, two-story portion of the house was built a few years later to accommodate a tavern that served teamsters traveling back and forth between the Erie Canal in Pittsford village and the mills of Honeoye Falls. A large ballroom occupied the entire front of the second floor. When the tavern failed in 1831, the building became a residence, serving as the

home of the Truman F. Smith family from 1836 to 1908. The first floor originally had an open porch with columns, which supported a second floor overhang. This porch, now enclosed, obscures the original facade.

Continue south on Mendon Center Road for about two miles to the four-way stop at the inter-section of Rt. 251, in the hamlet of Mendon Center. During the 19th-century, the hamlet was an active trading center for area farmers, includ-ing thrifty Quakers who settled the rich farmland. Go straight onto Rt. 251 (Rush-Mendon Center Road).

The next two houses are difficult to see, but worth making the effort. Although their addresses are on different roads, they are actually across the street from one another. The handsome, board-and-batten Gothic Revival house on the right, at **388 Mendon Center Road**, was constructed in at least two stages. The north section was built using hand-hewn post-and-beam construction methods prevalent in the 1830s. In the 1860s, the house was enlarged by William Cox, a wealthy banker and farmer, whose son William Wasson Cox was a well-known carriage painter and artist.

On the left is a stately Greek Revival house, at **3277 Rush-Mendon Road**, which can best be seen by parking on the shoulder of the road just beyond the driveway of No. 388 and just before the stand of evergreen trees. George A. Turner and his brother, Charles, occupied an earlier two-story house, which was destroyed by fire in 1826. In 1857, the Turner brothers rebuilt their home to its present appearance. This two-story frame house features a handsome recessed entrance with fluted columns, as well as colonnaded side porch. Once known as Locust Grove Farm, the property still retains a number of historic barns and outbuildings, as well as several surviving locust trees. For many years, this house and 183 acres of land were the property of Edward H. White, a Quaker, prominent farmer, and public official, having served as Justice of the Peace, town supervisor, and state assemblyman.

As you continue on Rush-Mendon Road, you'll pass Quaker Meeting House Road on the left where the Friends' Society built a meeting house (no longer extant) in 1832.

Before turning left onto Clover Street (Route 65), notice the large cobblestone house on the far corner, at **4389 Clover Street**. Luther Gates built the residence in 1834, but the house had greater significance under the ownership of the Cornells, a Quaker family, who opened it for Quaker meetings during the mid-19th century. The building is another Mendon cobblestone listed in the National Register of Historic Places. Its white-painted stone quoins, lintels and sills, as well as the solid stone jambs around both doorways, stand out against the multi-colored fieldstones. The front wraparound porch, with its cast-concrete block foundation, is a modern addition.

On the left, at **4420 Clover Street**, set at an angle behind large pine trees is a Greek Revival house once known as the Sherwood-Douglas house. Built in 1855, it originally stood on Douglas Road in Mendon Ponds Park. For many years, it served as the park superintendent's residence, and when it was deemed surplus by park officials, it was slated for demolition. After its architectural and historic significance was confirmed, it was moved to this site in 1980 and is now a private residence.

Sibleyville

Continuing on south Clover Street, we drive past Sibley Road, just before entering the village of Honeoye Falls. At the west end of this road was the 19th-century hamlet of Sibleyville. It was there that pioneer Hiram Sibley began his rise to prominence. Here, he built mills and manufactured farming implements, which eventually helped provide the funds to establish Western Union Telegraph Company (see Chapter 1). His 1827 house still stands at 29 Sibley Road and is listed in the National Register of Historic Places.

Nearby on Plains Road was the 17th-century Seneca Indian village of Totiakton. The village was one of four Seneca villages in the area identified by the explorer Wentworth Greenhalge in 1677. At that time, about 1,000 people lived there, and it was the second largest of four Seneca villages; the nearby village at Ganondagan in Victor was the largest (see sidebar on Ganondagan).

In 1687, the Marquis Denonville, governor of the French Colony New France (Canada), ravaged Totiakton on a mission of destruction, which also devastated the village at Ganondagan. His actions were part of a long-standing conflict between his colony and the area's native Americans. As the Frenchman marched through Seneca territory with an army of 2,000 men, Seneca scouts warned their fellow villagers of Denonville's approach, Forewarned, the Senecas had already deserted their towns and burned their homes by the time he arrived. Denonville's men cut down corn and burned crops, but the Senecas rebuilt their villages elsewhere after the invasion. Although Denonville is known as a destroyer in western New York, he was criticized in his own era, and later for his failure to inflict greater punishment on native people during his attack. At the end of his term as governor (according to the 1908 *Catholic Encyclopedia*), "he was looked upon as lacking in ability to deal with the savages," and criticized for allowing native people "too much liberty."

Although there are no physical remains of Totiakton, Ganondagan, in the nearby town of Victor, has been declared a National Historic Landmark and is now a New York State Historic Site open to the public.

Ganondagan

Ganondagan can be reached at the end of the tour by taking a right on East Street (in the village of Honeoye Falls), which becomes Boughton Hill Road. Proceed east about nine miles until you come to Ganondagan State Historic Site, located on the left, just before the intersection of Victor-Holcomb Road at the flashing red light.

Ganondagan was occupied by the Senecas at the same time as Totiakton, and destroyed during the same Denonville mission in 1687. Before its destruction, it was regarded as a prosperous Seneca village, with four tall storehouses of corn and 150 longhouses. By the late 1700s, when white settlers began cultivating the land, the area was virtually all fields and pastures.

During the late-19th and early-20th centuries, Ganondagan was pillaged by archaeologists and looters, who removed artifacts and skeletal remains. Beginning in 1945, local historian Sheldon Fisher and Arthur Parker, a Seneca and an archaeologist who was director of the Rochester Museum of Arts and Sciences (now the Rochester Museum and Science Center), sought to stop the desecration of the site.

In 1964, Ganondagan was declared a National Historic Landmark. New York State succeeded in purchasing more than 300 acres of the area, and on July 14, 1987, the site was formally dedicated, 300 years to the day after Denonville destroyed the town.

Today, the former Seneca village site features a reconstructed bark longhouse, a visitor's center, and hiking trails at its hilltop location. The 17th-century bark longhouse, measuring 65' long, 20' wide and 20' high, contains handmade Native American objects, along with European trade items, which help present an accurate portrayal of Seneca life during the fur-trade era. The marked trails detail Seneca history and traditions, identify plants used by the Senecas, and provide insight into the Denonville campaign.

Honeoye Falls – "Where the Finger Lies"

Clover Street leads directly into the village of Honeoye Falls. "Honeoye" stems from a Seneca word meaning "where the finger lies," or "finger lying there." One of several legends of the word's origin has it that two men were fighting, and one wrapped his hand around a sapling as he hid behind a larger tree. During the battle, one of his fingers was severed when his opponent threw a tomahawk at him. Continuing to fight though he was in pain, the man with the severed finger went on to win the battle. When he told others of the battle, he talked about the place where "the little finger lies on the ground."

Honeoye Creek, with its scenic waterfalls, has been the focus of village life since 1791, when Zebulon Norton first erected a grist mill on the west bank of the upper falls. His small settlement, known as Norton's Mills, grew to be a self-supporting community during the early 19th century. By 1838, it was incorporated as the village of Honeoye Falls. During the second half of the 19th century, the village expanded as rail transportation facilitated the trade of the area's agricultural products to new urban markets.

The placid suburban village of Honeoye Falls is a quieter place today than it was in years past. Its earlier prominence as a center of commercial, industrial and social activity, however, is reflected in its historic architecture. Most of the village is a designated historic district listed in the National Register of Historic Places.

The first sign that you are entering a former mill town is evident after crossing over Honeoye Creek. On the left is the towering **Lower Mill at 61 North Main Street**. Built in the 1830s by Hiram Finch as a flour mill, the building is constructed of stone that was quarried just northwest of the site. After a fire gutted the building's interior in 1901, it was quickly rebuilt with new equipment and continued as a flour mill, with 150 barrels of flour a day shipped to France during World War I. Today, the building's beamed interior has been adapted for artistic venues.

Continuing along North Main Street, you'll find several representative examples of the 19th-century residential architecture found throughout the village, which include Federal, Greek Revival, Italianate, Queen Anne and other styles.

The handsome white, temple-style church on the left at **27 North Main Street** is the Greek Revival-style First Presbyterian Church, one of three significant historic churches in the village. For a closer look, turn left just past the church at the entrance to the park with the gazebo. This is an ideal place to park and view the village on foot, or simply to park while looking at nearby buildings from the car. The church edifice, erected in 1842, features four massive Doric columns and a square, two-tiered classical tower. The Presbyterian church was established in 1831 in a small frame meeting house. When the congregation grew, the original church building was sold to the local Baptists who moved it to the banks of the creek. They later sold the small church back to the Presbyterians, who incorporated it into the southeast corner of the present structure.

The village park, known as **Harry Allen Park**, was named after a village founding father and physician, who deeded the park to the community. In 1838, Allen was declared the first mayor (then called president) of the village of Honeoye Falls. Early in the 19th century, animals had free rein of the larger village, until an 1838 village ordinance called for a picket fence to be erected around the present park to keep "horses, cattle, swine and geese from running at large."

The park is distinguished by three notable structures. The gazebo in the middle of the park was built in 1988 on the site of a bandstand that stood for years. The park also was the site of an early brick schoolhouse, demolished in 1928. Today, located in the back of the park is the former **Mendon District No. 15 Schoolhouse**, now a museum owned and maintained by the **Honeoye Falls-Town of Mendon Historical Society**. This compact one-room schoolhouse once served a single teacher with an average of 11 students in grades 1 through 7. Built about 1895-1900 and in use until 1944, the schoolhouse was moved to the park in 1991. Inside, the museum contains benches in rows, an old map and a teacher's desk, and provides a living history experience for today's schoolchildren. The Honeoye Falls-Town of Mendon Historical Society also owns the large board-and-batten **Thompson Building**. Built in 1860 as a carriage barn and livery stable for the former Falls Hotel at 1 North Main Street, the building serves as a museum and is open to the public.

Exit the park and turn left back onto Main Street. At the main village intersection on the left, at **1 North Main Street**, is the three-story, painted brick "**Masonic Temple**." Formerly called the Wilcox House, this building originally was a mid-19th-century hotel that catered to travelers who stopped in this busy village. The first hotel at this location was built in 1812, and its foundation can still be seen from the nearby bridge. In 1827, the earliest portion of the existing building was erected as the two-story Falls Hotel. The Federal front door with transom and sidelights dates from the period. In 1861, the building was enlarged with the addition of the third story and the wide decorative brick cornice.

At the light, turn left onto East Street to cross over Honeoye Creek and to view the falls and the prominent stone **Upper Mill** on the right. Once a source of power for the early industries of the village, today, the stream and attractive mill pond serve as a scenic and recreational resource.

Sitting on the opposite bank of the creek, at **5 East Street**, is the handsome, brick, Romanesque Revival **Village Hall**. Built in 1886 and designed by the Rochester architectural firm of Fay and Dryer, the building is one of the most distinctive

Masonic Temple   *Padelt*

village halls in Monroe County. Until 1945, it housed the Honeoye Falls Fire Department, and the hose-drying tower still remains in the southeast corner. A large auditorium on the second floor originally was used for theater productions. The four-story bell tower, featuring large arched windows and an arched belfry, is crowned by the locally famous "Iron Fireman." The five-foot-high, painted metal fireman figure in blue pants and a red top and blowing a "fireman's horn," is a village landmark and a reminder of a long-standing rivalry between local fire departments. Created in the early 1800s for the St. Catharines, Ontario, fire department, the ornament was left in Rochester by accident after a convention. It soon became the object of good-natured thievery between fire departments in the area. Using hacksaw blades, Honeoye Falls snatched the fireman in October 1891 from the Avon fire hall. Ultimately, it was mounted on the Village Hall, where it remained until 1999 when it became too fragile for its rooftop display. In 2000, a replica was installed on the tower, replacing the original folk art figure, which now is exhibited inside.

Continuing straight on East Street are reminders of the village's past carriage-making industries. The first distinctive house on the right, at **19 East Street**, is the Queen Anne-style residence of carriage-maker James Elliott, whose shop building still stands next door. Opposite, at **No. 26**, is the three-story frame former Druschel Carriage Works.

Turn right onto Church Street. The red brick and stone **United Methodist Church**, on the corner of East and Church streets, has been well preserved and maintained since its erection in 1874. The buttressed bell tower and the arched stone detailing on the doorways and windows are noteworthy.

Turn right onto Ontario Street and pull over to the side of the road opposite Nos. 39 and 37. A fashionable haven in the late 1800s and early 1900s, this street features an impressive cluster of Queen Anne houses that is lively and colorful. The highly decorative house, at **39 Ontario Street**, was built in 1890 by the Methodist church to house its minister. The ornamental woodwork on the two-story front porch and in the upper gable ends reflects the earlier Eastlake style.

Next door, the large Eastlake-style house at **37 Ontario Street** is one of the best-known and architecturally noteworthy houses in the village. Built in 1885, the house was constructed for Richard Peer, a businessman who sold carriages, wagons and cutters from a shop on East Street. Its picturesque composition includes a front gable balcony with a projecting roof and stick-work railings, machine-cut verge boards, and decorative shingles, which also serve as small roofs over the first-floor windows.

Also distinctive is the asymmetrical, hipped-roof Queen Anne on the left, at **29 Ontario Street**. Built about 1884, the house features a projecting main gable on the front with an unusual solid gable detail and brackets. Also notice the original carriage house in the rear, which has been well preserved.

The large, brick Greek Revival house, on the left at **23 Ontario Street**, was a grand and expensive building for the late 1830s and early 1840s when it was built. Colonel Henry Culver, builder of the Upper Mill, started construction but met with "financial reverses," leaving Hiram Finch, builder of the Lower Mill, to spend as much as

29 Ontario Street   *Petronio*

$20,000 to finish the project, which was then dubbed "Finch's Folly." The building later served as a home for doctors, and as a hospital during World War II.

Turn left on East Street, cross the creek, and turn left onto West Main Street. On the right, at **1 West Main Street**, is the **Wilcox-Dann Building**, a handsome Victorian commercial block, built in 1882, and constructed with a reported 200,000 bricks. Framing the first-floor commercial storefronts are cast-iron pilasters.

Turn left into the Mendon Town Hall parking lot, just past the stone Upper Mill. The massive stone **Upper Mill**, at **16 West Main Street**, was built in 1827 by Colonel Henry Culver on the site of Zebulon Norton's first grist mill, erected in 1791. It was then sold to Hiram Finch who later built the Lower Mill. Like the Lower Mill, the building is constructed of dolomite stone quarried from Honeoye Creek. The mill produced flour from 1827 to 1963, including a period during World War II when it operated 24 hours a day, converting six train cars of wheat into 450 barrels of flour per day to meet wartime demand. In the 1980s, after briefly serving as a restaurant, the building became the Mendon Town Hall.

Looking across the creek, on the opposite bank, is the frame **Ritzenthaler Sawmill**. It was built on the site where Zebulon Norton constructed his sawmill in the 1790s. The lower stone floors may still retain masonry from Norton's original building. The exposed buttresses in the middle and on the edge of the creek represent the trestle remnants of the New York Central Railroad.

Across the street is the distinctive, golden-colored brick former **Bank of Honeoye Falls**, at **31 West Main Street**. It is a fine example of the Classical Revival style of the late 1890s when it was constructed. Look for the semi-circular shell motifs over the second-story windows.

Leave the parking lot and turn right onto Main Street and left onto Episcopal Avenue next to the bank building. This leads directly to **St. John's Episcopal Church**, the village's third historic church and individually listed in the National Register of Historic Places. Built in 1841-42 of local dolomite stone, also quarried from the nearby creek, the church is distinctive for its Greek Revival temple-style portico, combined with Gothic Revival elements that include pointed-arched windows and louvered openings in the bell tower. Cosseted in a park-like setting, the structure is known as "The Church Among the Trees," and is complemented by the survival of its original carriage shed, now used as the church office.

Turn around and return to West Main Street, taking a right turn to look at the final residential grouping of this tour. The Second Empire house at **51 West Main Street**, built c. 1850, is a fine representative of the style, featuring a slate mansard roof, a distinctive porch with large brackets supporting the roof, and smaller decorative brackets under the eaves, on the front bay window and the side porch.

The house at **55 West Main Street** is an architectural hybrid. In the rear of the 1890s three-story Queen Anne front portion is the original one-and-a-half-story Greek Revival house built c. 1850 on the site. You can spot the tell-tale Greek Revival frieze windows on the earlier house.

You can continue on West Main Street to admire more fine residences of mid-to-late-19th century and to test your knowledge of architectural styles you've seen on this tour. Before returning to Rochester, turn around and take a minute, if possible, and go back to the parking lot next to the Mendon Town Hall. The dense forest that enabled two young Senecas to fight near the falls is no longer present, and the railroads are long gone. Yet one can imagine the noisy churning of Zebulon Norton's grist and saw mills, or the barrels of flour being loaded on railroad cars. Honeoye Falls is a village defined by its rich historic surroundings and its natural beauty, which remain for visitors and residents to appreciate.

You can now return to Rochester. Or, if you wish, you can drive to Ganondagan in Victor (for directions see sidebar).

Wilson Commons, University of Rochester, by I.M. Pei   *Petronio*

Modern Style: architecture
using new materials in new applications,
celebrating structure, and avoiding the use of
redundant ornamental and historical motifs.

Of all architectural styles, that which we call
'modern' may be the most paradoxical. While
modern has positive connotations in most areas—
medicine, automobiles, and appliances—modern
architecture has been slow to gain long-term
public acceptance, even enduring criticism
within the architectural profession itself.
Although modern design attained brief post-
war dominance with home-buyers and designers,
more recent times have witnessed a near stam-
pede to embrace the architectural forms, if not
the technology, of the past.

Pioneers in the modern movement resisted
the very idea of a modern 'style'; this seemingly
equivocated their efforts with those of the past,
while they felt that the new architecture was the
only rational choice. Nonetheless, thanks to

the 1932 Museum of Modern Art exhibit and monograph, *The International Style: Architecture Since 1922*, the modern movement in architecture was well on its way to being an identifiable style by the early 1930s.

Modern architecture has both domestic and foreign sources. American architects like Frank Furness, Henry Hobson Richardson, Louis Sullivan, Greene and Greene and Frank Lloyd Wright all were associated with modern ideas. Modernism's foreign lineage involved LeCorbusier, Richard Neutra, Walter Gropius, Eliel and Eero Saarinen, William Lescaze, Alvar Alto and Mies van der Rohe. Many European modernists emigrated to America before World War II, and after the War, the domestic and foreign aspects of modernism became less distinct.

Similarly, Rochester has produced modern works by both native and imported talent. Andrew J. and J. Foster Warner, Harvey Ellis, Claude Bragdon and Gordon and Kaelber were Rochester architects of the 19th and early-20th centuries whose work paralleled national leaders. Out-of-town notables Frank Lloyd Wright and William Lescaze had both designed houses in Rochester by 1940, and later, Pietro Belluschi,

Louis Kahn, Victor Gruen, Edward L. Barnes, Roche-Dinkeloo, Skidmore Owings and Merrill, Richard Meier, I. M. Pei and James S. Polshek contributed to Rochester's architectural heritage.

Since Rochester was a fairly early adopter of modern architectural ideas, the area retains several buildings from the 1930s which illustrate characteristics of the early modern International Style. Good examples of the more decorative Art Deco and Art Moderne styles survive also, and the region retains numerous homes and commercial buildings that were obviously influenced by purer modern examples here and abroad.

Modernism represents a new frontier for preservationists as well. Since each generation seems least appreciative of the styles immediately preceding its own, modern buildings are often under-appreciated regardless of quality, and thus are threatened by our own time. Fortunately, some Rochester area municipalities have recognized this problem, and have designated a number of Art Moderne and International Style buildings as local landmarks, affording them at least the protection of local preservation boards.

James Yarrington, AIA
LSWNY President 1997/98

Sources

Landmarks of Rochester and Monroe County, by Paul Malo (Syracuse University Press, 1974)

Rochester Historical Society Publication Fund Series, volumes I-XXV, 1922-1972

Rochester History Series, Rochester city historian, Rochester Public Library, 1939-present

Elegant Village, Architecture Worth Saving in Pittsford, Andrew D. Wolfe (Phoenix Press; 1969)

"Genesee River Tryptych," videotape written and narrated by Bill Davis, Charlotte-Genesee Lighthouse Historical Society

George Eastman, by Elizabeth Brayer (The John Hopkins University Press, 1996)

The Towpath, by Arch Merrill (L. Heindl and Son, 1945)

Rochester ... (four-volume history), by Blake McKelvey (Harvard University Press, 1945, 1949, 1956; Christopher Press, 1961)

Rochester and Monroe County, Federal Writer's Project (Scantom's, 1937)

"Lake Avenue," by Sean Kirst, *City* newspaper, April 5, 1984

Frederick Law Olmsted, Designing the American Landscape, by Charles E. Beveridge and Paul Rocheleau (Rizzoli, 1995)

"Memories of Childhood at Warner Castle," by Ruth Van Deusen, *University of Rochester Library Bulletin*, Autumn 1975

Runnin' Crazy: A Portrait of the Genesee River, by Ruth Rosenberg-Naparsteck with Edward P. Curtis Jr., (The Donning Company, 1996)

Other Sources, Chapter One: *A History of the Town of Brighton 1814-1989*, by the 175th Anniversary Committee; *A Short History of Pittsford*, by Audrey M. Johnson; *West Brighton Folk and Lore*, by Margaret McNab

Chapter Two: *History of Charlotte*, by Emma M. Pollard Greer and Carlos deZafra, Jr., ed., 1977, Charlotte Community Association;

"Historical Souvenir of the Valley of the Genesee," by Elon Huntington Hooker, presented at the dinner of the Society of the Genesee, New York City, Jan. 23, 1933; *History of Monroe County*, 1877. Phila: Everts, Ensign and Everts; Vol. II, No. 2; "St. Bernard's Semininary: Ghosts in the Corridors," by Emily Morrison, *Courier Journal* (undated); "Lake Avenue," by Sean Kirst, *City* newspaper, April 5, 1984

Chapter 3: "An Architect's House," by Claude Bragdon, *Good Housekeeping*, 1904; *"Bricksville Revisited,"* by Lawrence B. Anderson, Empire State Architect, Sept. 1972; "Mr. Eastman Builds a House, Part XXXV," by Betsy Brayer, *The Brighton-Pittsford Post*, clipping undated; "New York State History – Wheatland Area," by Shirley DiStefano; "Rochester's Olmstedian Public Pleasure Grounds," George Eastman House, 1999; "The RIT campus, A Microcosm of the Late Sixties," by Houghton Wetherald; "Seen and Heard," by Henry W. Clune, Rochester *Democrat and Chronicle*, Nov. 25, 1965; "Walking Tour of the Village of Scottsville," The Wheatland Historical Association; *A History of the University of Rochester*, by Arthur J. May (University of Rochester Press, 1977); "A Suitable and Worthy Architecture," *Rochester Review*, Fall 1980, by Jean R. France

Chapter Four: "150 Years in Ogden, 100 Years in Spencerport," Earl Edgar White, 1967; "From Spencerport's Star Corner, the 'Village building,'" by Paul Humphrey; "Town of Clarkson Sesquicentennial," 1969; "Town of Sweden Sesquicentennial Celebration," 1964; "Walking Tour of Brockport," date and author unknown;

Chapter Five: *A Country School Goes to Town*, by Diane C. Ham; *A Short History of Pittsford*, by Audrey M. Johnson; Historical Map of Pittsford, A Walking Tour Map, Historic Pittsford, Inc.; Honeoye Falls, NY – Its Beginning, by David K. Maloney, 1963; "Pioneer Burying Ground," and "The Phoenix Falls and Rises," Historic Pittsford, March 2000; The Flavor of Honeoye Falls 1838-1988, by Anne Bullock; "The Ghosts of Sawmills and Rowdy Railroad Men," Susan Tew, Home Guide – Wolfe Publications, March 10, 1980; Town of Mendon, Sesquicentennial Souvenir Program and History, by Amo T. Kreiger, 1963; *Walking Tour, Historic District of Honeoye Falls*, date and author unknown.

Notes

Notes

About the Photographers

Andy Olenick, a graduate of Rochester Institute of Technology's photography program, created the superb photos for the books, *200 Years of Rochester Architecture and Gardens*, *Classic Buffalo – A Heritage of Distinguished Architecture* and *Erie Canal Legacy*. His studio – Fotowerks, Inc. – is in Rochester's former city morgue (c. 1900), which he has restored to more lively pursuits.

The late Hans Padelt, inventor of the Graflex-XL camera, began his career in Dresden, Germany, where he was a camera designer and professional photographer. From 1951 to 1969, he was senior engineer at the Graflex Company in Rochester and produced the outstanding photographs for the Landmark Society's first book, *Landmarks of Rochester and Monroe County*.

Dawn Tower, another graduate of Rochester Institute of Technology's photography program, is a professor of photography and an architectural photographer based in Rochester.

Frank Petronio, this book's designer, is also a prolific photographer. His design studio creates publications, corporate identities, advertising and web sites for both large and small companies. He often creates the photos and images used in his designs. You can learn more about Frank by visiting his website at www.frankpetronio.com.

These photographers donated the usage of their photographs in this book. All of the images are copyrighted by their respective photographers, and should not be reproduced without permission.

Additional Titles
by the Landmark Society of Western New York

200 Years of Rochester Architecture and Gardens, 144 pages, 180 full-color photos, large format, hardcover. Photographer Andy Olenick and writer Richard Reisem ($39.95).

The Rochester Jazz Collection ~ Landmarks in Music, CD of the best music of Rochester greats; Chuck and Gap Mangione, Cab Calloway, Jeff Tyzik and others ($15.98).

Mount Hope Cemetery — America's First Municipal Victorian Cemetery, 128 pages, large format, hardcover. Text by Richard Reisem and photography by Frank Gillespie ($39.95).

The City of Frederick Douglass: Rochester's African-American People and Places, 50 pages, softcover, by Eugene E. Du Bois ($6.95).

Images of History: Walking Tours of Downtown Rochester, 50 pages, six walking tours with maps and photos, softcover and wire-bound ($4.95).

Rehab Rochester: A Sensible Guide for Old-House Maintenance, Repair, and Rehabilitation, 96 pages, softcover, by Steve Jordan; illustrations by Melissa Carlson ($9.95).

Erie Canal Legacy — Architectural Treasures of the Empire State, 208 pages, 300 full-color photos, photographer Andy Olenick and writer Richard Reisem ($39.95).

Songs of the Erie Canal, CD, a tuneful variety of historic songs by the world-famous Irish duo, The Dady Brothers ($15.98).

Photographer Andy Olenick and writer Richard Reisem have spent over a decade researching and recording the historic treasures of western New York. Their other collaboration, *Classic Buffalo — A Heritage of Distinguished Architecture*, (which was designed by Frank Petronio) was published by Canisius College Press.

Visit www.landmarksociety.org
or call us at 1 (888) 546-3849